in a
snap!

Tasty Southern Recipes
YOU CAN MAKE IN
5, 10, 15, or 30 Minutes

Tammy Algood

THOMAS NELSON
Since 1798

NASHVILLE   DALLAS   MEXICO CITY   RIO DE JANEIRO

Published in Nashville, Tennessee, by Thomas Nelson. Thomas Nelson is a registered trademark of Thomas Nelson, Inc.

Photography by Mark Boughton

Food Styling by Teresa Blackburn

Page design by Lori Lynch

Thomas Nelson, Inc., titles may be purchased in bulk for educational, business, fund-raising, or sales promotional use. For information, please e-mail SpecialMarkets@ThomasNelson.com.

Library of Congress Cataloging-in-Publication Data

Algood, Tammy.
 In a snap! : tasty Southern recipes you can make in 5, 10, 15, or 30 minutes / Tammy Algood.
    pages cm
 Includes bibliographical references and index.
 ISBN 978-1-4016-0486-8 (pbk.)
 1. Cooking, American—Southern style. 2. Quick and easy cooking. I. Algood, Tammy. II. Title.
 TX715.2.S68A393 2013
 641.5975—dc23   2012041461

Printed in the United States of America

13 14 15 16 17 QG 6 5 4 3 2

Contents

Introduction

I have to admit that I loved a class I had in college called Meal Management. It was all about timing: getting recipes that cooked at different temperatures and for various lengths of time to the table at the same time. I don't even know if that class is taught anymore, but I honestly use some of what I learned there practically every time I prepare a meal.

Time certainly remains in the forefront of the minds of those who feed families today. One of the biggest challenges facing any weeknight cook is getting food on the table fast, so it can be eaten even faster. Numerous hindrances like homework, housework, yard work, and work from your job can get in the way of spending time on more enjoyable things. Unfortunately, good food and being together as a family at the table often get sacrificed.

Most will save their "real cooking" for the weekends or for special occasions and holidays. If this has become your routine, this cookbook is designed to change that habit. *In a Snap!* is your easiest path to those happy words, "Time to eat!" It will help you realize that incredibly tasty Southern food *can* be served to your family on practically any hurried morning or harried night of the week.

The key to making this cookbook useable for me was to showcase and utilize food items that are both readily available and affordable. There are fantastic food gems hidden away at the supermarket, in your freezer, and even pushed to the back of your pantry. These can find a lovely home in all sorts of dishes that will satisfy your family while keeping your food budget right on target.

The recipes are divided so you can match the dish with the amount of time you have available. Maybe you want to spend more time eating with your family than cooking. Not a problem! Just go to the 5-, 10-, and 15-minute sections. If you have a bit more time to spend, then flip to those recipes that can be done in 30 minutes. All of them count on uncomplicated cooking techniques to keep things easy. Fussy, tedious foods take a back seat here, but that doesn't mean these dishes are not beautiful when simply garnished and served.

To keep things easy, always completely read the recipe before you begin any preparation or cooking. Then you won't have any surprises and will have a good idea of the steps for completion. Also, it helps to gather all the ingredients you will need before you start cooking. Often, you can prepare items needed later in the recipe while things are boiling or cooking. That can be an extremely helpful tool for saving valuable time.

Every effort has been made to account for various speed skills as far as jobs like chopping, peeling, and slicing are concerned. The times indicated for each of the recipes use knife skills, but don't hesitate to put great kitchen tools like food processors to work. Once you get used to the various blades and attachments, you'll find that it will quickly become your most valued kitchen assistant.

So whether you need a quick appetizer because of drop-by guests, a delicious side dish to carry to an impromptu neighborhood gathering, or a speedy soup and salad to enjoy after a long day away from home, it's all here. And with just a few twists and turns in your kitchen, you've got down-home, wholesome dishes that are suddenly family favorites and on the table *In a Snap!*

5 Minutes

Country Ham Spread

I love experimenting with various dips, sauces, and spreads. I call this a spread because it is a bit thicker than others. I love serving it with sweet, sturdy carrot sticks or crisp celery stalks that can hold up to the weight of the spread. It also makes a terrific substitute for mayonnaise on your next tomato sandwich.

Yield: 2 cups

1 ½ cups mayonnaise

½ cup ground country ham*

3 tablespoons chicken or vegetable stock

1 teaspoon white wine
   Worcestershire sauce

1 teaspoon garlic powder

1 teaspoon dry mustard

¼ teaspoon dried onions

¼ teaspoon hot sauce

In a mixing bowl, stir together the mayonnaise, ham, stock, Worcestershire sauce, garlic powder, dry mustard, onions, and hot sauce. Serve immediately, or cover and refrigerate for later use.

STORAGE NOTE: *Because of the mayonnaise, this recipe cannot be frozen. Store leftovers in the refrigerator for up to 5 days.*

*You can find ground country ham at places that sell country ham and at really good meat markets. Or you can ask your supermarket meat manager at your local store to grind it for you as soon as you buy it, or grind it at home for just the right quantity.

🕑 *Time-Saving Tip from Tammy*

Appetizers are a fun way to begin any party, but how much food do you need? If it is going to be an appetizer party with no meal, then plan on 6 to 8 appetizer servings per person. If the appetizers are soon going to be followed by a meal, allow between 2 and 4 appetizer servings per guest. If it will be quite a bit of time between the appetizers and the meal, allow 4 to 6 servings per person.

We're Hungry Cheese Dip

You've heard it before . . . "We're starving!" Well, take care of that declaration without ruining dinner with this easy cheese dip. Serve it with carrot sticks, celery stalks, mushrooms, pretzel sticks, or bagel chips. Adults will like it with meatballs.

Yield: 1 ½ cups

1 (10-ounce) can cheddar cheese soup   **½ cup chicken stock**

Whisk together the soup and stock in a glass mixing bowl. Cover with waxed paper and microwave on high power for 30 seconds. Whisk again to evenly combine. If needed, heat for another 15 seconds. Serve warm.

STORAGE NOTE: Leftovers should be refrigerated and used within 3 days. Do not freeze.

Green Onion Spread

This lively spread is terrific on low-salt crackers and pairs well with any raw vegetables. Leftovers make a great morning bagel spread.

Yield: 1 ¼ cups

2 garlic cloves, peeled

6 ounces cream cheese, softened

½ cup cottage cheese

2 teaspoons dried parsley

⅛ teaspoon seasoned salt

⅛ teaspoon white pepper

⅛ teaspoon cayenne

1 green onion, chopped

Place the garlic in a food processor and mince. Add the cream cheese, cottage cheese, parsley, seasoned salt, white pepper, and cayenne. Process until smooth. Transfer to a serving bowl and stir in the green onions. Serve with assorted crackers and vegetables.

STORAGE NOTE: Store leftovers in the refrigerator and use within 4 days. Do not freeze.

Payday Party Mix

This recipe from my friend Bryan gives you a big payoff for just a bit of effort. At first, I was skeptical when he shared it with me, but then I served it at a party and it was gone in a flash! It will earn rave reviews from your guests.

Yield: 12 servings

1 (16-ounce) jar roasted peanuts (lightly salted)

1 (22-ounce) bag candy corn

Place the peanuts in a large serving bowl. Add the candy corn and lightly mix to distribute evenly in the bowl. Serve.

STORAGE NOTE: *Place leftovers in any type of air-tight container and store at room temperature.*

Red Pepper Cheese Dip

*This creamy dip can be pulled together at the last minute
and served with tortilla, corn, or pita chips.*

Yield: 1 ½ cups

1 (8-ounce) package cream cheese
1 tablespoon milk or half-and-half

**½ cup canned, chopped, roasted
sweet red bell peppers**
½ cup crumbled Feta cheese

Place the cream cheese in a glass bowl and microwave on high power for 20 seconds to soften. Add the milk, bell peppers, and Feta cheese. Microwave for 20 to 30 seconds longer and stir to blend. Serve immediately.

*STORAGE NOTE: Store leftovers in the refrigerator
and use within 5 days. Do not freeze.*

White Cheese Lovers Dipping Sauce

In addition to a terrific chip dip, this delicious sauce can be poured over steamed veggies or even leftover noodles or rice. If you have leftovers, heat on low power in the microwave for 30-second time increments, stirring frequently until heated through.

Yield: 4 servings

1 tablespoon unsalted butter

1 tablespoon all-purpose flour

⅛ teaspoon white pepper

¾ cup milk

½ cup shredded Monterey Jack cheese

½ cup shredded Gouda or Havarti

In a 4-cup microwaveable measuring cup, melt the butter on high power in the microwave for 10 seconds. Stir in the flour and pepper, and microwave for 10 seconds longer. Stir in the milk and microwave for 2 minutes or until just boiling. Stop and stir after 1 minute. Gradually add the Monterey Jack and Gouda, stirring until completely melted. If necessary, microwave for 30 seconds longer. Serve immediately.

Note: You can substitute Swiss, Gruyère, or Fontina for the Gouda if desired.

Storage Note: The cheese will tend to separate and dry out when frozen, so instead, refrigerate and use within 5 days.

Spiced Cranberry Dipping Sauce

*Got leftover turkey or chicken strips? Even if you don't, purchase
some already cooked for dunking into this yummy sauce.*

Yield: 1 ⅓ cups

1 cup cranberry sauce

⅓ cup taco sauce

1 canned chipotle pepper, minced

1 teaspoon chili powder

½ teaspoon ground cumin

¼ teaspoon salt

¼ teaspoon white pepper

Place the cranberry sauce, taco sauce, pepper, chili powder, cumin, salt, and white pepper in a glass bowl and microwave on high power for 1 minute. Stir and microwave for another 30 seconds. Stir again and serve warm or at room temperature.

*STORAGE NOTE: This recipe freezes extremely well. Use within
6 months. Refrigerated leftovers will keep up to a week.*

Tickle Your Tongue Mustard Dip

*Pretzels and chicken strips never had it so good. Use leftovers
as a spread for bologna, ham, or turkey sandwiches.*

Yield: 1 cup

⅓ cup mayonnaise

⅓ cup Dijon mustard

1 ½ tablespoons prepared horseradish

1 tablespoon sugar

¼ teaspoon white pepper

In a glass bowl, whisk together the mayonnaise, mustard, horseradish, sugar, and pepper. Microwave on high power for 15 seconds. Stir and serve immediately.

*Storage Note: Leftovers should be refrigerated
and used within 1 week. Do not freeze.*

Sneaky Buttermilk Ranch Dressing

Your kids and family members will never guess what gives this homemade dressing its familiar taste. It's a terrific way to sneak beans into the meal!

Yield: 1 ¹/₂ cups

1 cup buttermilk

1 cup canned Northern beans, drained and rinsed

2 tablespoons sour cream

1 garlic clove, minced

1 tablespoon dried parsley

1 tablespoon grated Parmesan cheese

½ teaspoon onion salt

¼ teaspoon white pepper

⅛ teaspoon cayenne

Place the buttermilk, beans, sour cream, garlic, parsley, Parmesan, onion salt, pepper, and cayenne in the bowl of a food processor. Process until smooth. Serve immediately.

STORAGE NOTE: Cover and refrigerate leftovers and use within 1 week. Do not freeze.

Date Night Basic Vinaigrette (with options)

A simple salad of mixed greens and a few cherry tomatoes becomes something special when you serve it with your own dressing. In this case, it's a marvelously healthy vinaigrette that can be tailor-made to fit your mood and the ingredients you have on hand.

Yield: ½ cup

¼ cup olive or canola oil

3 tablespoons red or white wine vinegar

½ teaspoon salt

¼ teaspoon black pepper

Options:

For Poppy Seed Vinaigrette, add 1 tablespoon poppy seeds.

For Tarragon Vinaigrette, add 2 tablespoons chopped fresh tarragon.

For Chive Vinaigrette, add 2 tablespoons chopped fresh chives and 2 teaspoons honey.

For Citrus Vinaigrette, add 1 tablespoon grated citrus zest and 1 tablespoon honey.

For Dill Shallot Vinaigrette, add 2 tablespoons chopped fresh dill and 1 small shallot, peeled and chopped.

In a jar with a tight-fitting lid, combine the oil, vinegar, salt, pepper, and your choice of the optional ingredients. Shake to emulsify, and use immediately.

Storage Note: Refrigerate leftovers and use within 2 weeks. Make sure you shake well to emulsify the ingredients each time you use it. Do not freeze.

⏱ *Time-Saving Tip from Tammy*

Vinegar is a necessary ingredient in salad dressings, but it tends to draw water out of the cells of the lettuce, causing it to wilt quickly. For this reason, only dress salads right before serving and you'll have crisp, perky greens.

Chicken Corn Chowder with Pimientos

The problem with many canned soups is they lack color. This one gets an added pop from sliced pimientos and fresh chives.

Yield: 2 servings

1 (18.5-ounce) can chicken corn chowder
1 (2-ounce) jar sliced pimientos, drained
¼ cup milk

2 tablespoons fresh minced chives
1 tablespoon bacon bits

Place the chowder, pimientos, and milk in a medium bowl and cover with waxed paper. Microwave on high power for 2 to 3 minutes. Meanwhile, chop the chives and measure the bacon bits. Stir and sprinkle with the chives and bacon bits. Serve warm.

STORAGE NOTE: *Refrigerate leftovers and use within 3 days. Freeze for up to 6 weeks.*

🕐 *Time-Saving Tip from Tammy*

Soup leftovers last up to 3 days in the refrigerator or can be frozen to use within 6 weeks. Gallon- or quart-size zip-top bags take up less storage space in the freezer than hard containers. Label and date the outside, then fill. Lay the bags flat in the freezer until hard, then stack them to save space. To use, simply thaw in the refrigerator overnight and reheat in a pot on medium-low temperature.

Chicken Sausage Gumbo

Here's a fulfilling soup for two that will be warming you from the inside out as soon as you take that first sip.

Yield: 2 servings

1 (18.5-ounce) can chicken gumbo

1 cup cooked, sliced chicken sausage

¼ cup water or chicken stock

1 teaspoon hot sauce

Place the gumbo, sausage, water, and hot sauce in a medium bowl and cover with waxed paper. Microwave on high power for 2 ½ to 3 minutes. Stir and serve warm.

STORAGE NOTE: Refrigerate leftovers and use within 3 days. Freeze for up to 6 weeks.

Summertime Cucumber Salad

This cold salad is perfect for cooling down your family on hot summer days, especially when cucumbers are coming in like gangbusters. It's great with burgers from the grill for lunch or with grilled fish for dinner.

Yield: 2 to 4 servings

2 large cucumbers, shredded

⅓ cup sour cream

2 tablespoons chopped fresh chives

2 teaspoons lemon juice

½ teaspoon kosher salt

¼ teaspoon white pepper

Place the cucumbers in a medium mixing bowl and add the sour cream, chives, lemon juice, salt, and pepper. Toss to mix well, and serve immediately.

STORAGE NOTE: This recipe cannot be frozen. Refrigerate leftovers and use within 3 days.

Spring Greens with Raspberry Dressing

Plain spring greens get a lift from this remarkable dressing based on raspberries. It is beautiful and perfect for garden parties or celebrations honoring Mom!

Yield: 4 servings

¼ cup seedless raspberry jam

¼ cup cranberry-raspberry juice

3 tablespoons raspberry vinegar

2 tablespoons olive oil

½ teaspoon salt

⅛ teaspoon black pepper

3 cups fresh baby spinach

1 cup arugula

Place the jam, juice, vinegar, oil, salt, and pepper in a jar with a tight-fitting lid. Shake to emulsify. Place the spinach and arugula in a serving bowl and toss with the dressing. Serve immediately.

STORAGE NOTE: Refrigerate leftover dressing and use within 1 week. Do not freeze.

Better with Butter Corn

*Mixing two different types of canned corn seems totally natural when
you pull it all together with herbed butter. Serve this terrific side dish with
grilled pork or baked ham or give it to the kids with hot fish sticks.*

Yield: 5 servings

1 (11-ounce) can whole kernel
   or niblets corn, drained

1 (11-ounce) can creamed corn

1 tablespoon chopped fresh parsley

1 tablespoon chopped fresh chives

4 tablespoons unsalted butter

Place the whole kernel corn, creamed corn, parsley, and chives in a serving bowl and stir to combine. Dot with the butter and cover with waxed paper. Microwave on high power for 2 minutes. Stir again and serve immediately.

*STORAGE NOTE: Leftovers can be frozen and used within 1
month or refrigerated and used within 3 days.*

🕐 *Time-Saving Tip from Tammy*

A good pair of kitchen shears serves a cook well with many tasks. For instance, you can cut whole canned tomatoes right in the opened can for no-mess chopping. But my favorite trick is to place fresh herbs in a glass measuring cup and start snipping away in the container. You can immediately see how much you've chopped and it's ready to use.

Family Favorite Black-Eyed Peas

*Black-eyes are my all-time favorite member of the pea family, and I
love the ease of having them readily available in the canned form.
With just a few additions, this seems more lively and ready for serving
with hot cooked rice or just about any grilled or roasted meat.*

Yield: 4 servings

1 (15.8-ounce) can black-eyed peas

1 small shallot, peeled and chopped

1 heaping tablespoon bacon bits

½ teaspoon cayenne

¼ teaspoon black pepper

Place the peas, shallots, bacon bits, cayenne, and black pepper in a serving bowl
and stir to combine. Cover with waxed paper and microwave on high power for 2
minutes. Stir and serve immediately.

*STORAGE NOTE: Leftovers can be frozen and used within 1
month or refrigerated and used within 3 days.*

⏱ *Time-Saving Tip from Tammy*

Your rice is nearly ready, but the rest of the
meal is not. Never fear! Simply remove it
from the heat source and place a folded
kitchen towel between the lid and the pot.
As the rice continues to steam from the
heat, the excess moisture that causes it to
become sticky will be absorbed by the towel
instead.

Wok-Seared Spinach

*Because this is truly the most instant side dish, you'll toss the leaves with
a delicious seasoning before it heads into the wok to sear. Have everything
else in your meal prepared because this is ready in just minutes.*

Yield: 4 servings

1 pound spinach with stems

2 tablespoons canola oil

2 tablespoons soy sauce

1 tablespoon sesame oil

½ teaspoon sugar

½ teaspoon crushed red pepper

Preheat a large wok over high heat. Meanwhile, place the spinach in a large mixing bowl and drizzle with the canola oil, soy sauce, and sesame oil. Sprinkle with the sugar and red pepper. Toss gently to evenly coat, and add to the wok. Toss it quickly in the pan to evenly sear. Within 2 minutes, it will begin to wilt and is ready to serve.

*STORAGE NOTE: Leftovers should be refrigerated
and used within 2 days. Do not freeze.*

Peaches and Cream Hominy

I love a corn variety named Peaches and Cream. Pull back the husk and you've got a mixture of sweet yellow and white kernels. This hominy side dish mimics that without the hassle of shucking, removing silks, and boiling the harvest.

Yield: 6 servings

1 (15.5-ounce) can golden
  hominy, drained

1 (15.5-ounce) can white hominy, drained

2 tablespoons unsalted butter

¼ teaspoon white pepper

Place the golden hominy, white hominy, butter, and pepper in a medium bowl and stir to combine. Cover with waxed paper and microwave on high power for 2 minutes. Stir and serve warm.

Storage Note: Leftovers can be frozen and used within 1 month or refrigerated and used within 3 days.

Show-Off Pinto Beans

*Spice up a can of reduced-sodium pinto beans, and you've got
a terrific side dish to serve with leftover cornbread.*

Yield: 4 servings

1 (16-ounce) can reduced-
sodium pinto beans

1 green onion, sliced

1 garlic clove, minced

½ teaspoon cayenne

¼ teaspoon white pepper

Place the beans, onions, garlic, cayenne, and white pepper in a serving bowl and stir
to combine. Cover with waxed paper and microwave on high power for 2 minutes.
Stir and serve immediately.

*STORAGE NOTE: Leftovers can be frozen and used within 1
month or refrigerated and used within 3 days.*

Dressed-Up Lima Beans

Canned vegetables come to the rescue for dinner side dishes. Serve with chicken, turkey, or ham.

Yield: 3 servings

1 (15-ounce) can lima beans, drained and rinsed

1 tablespoon bacon drippings or unsalted butter

1 small garlic clove, minced

½ teaspoon dried onions

¼ teaspoon black pepper

⅛ teaspoon sugar

Place the lima beans, bacon drippings, garlic, onions, pepper, and sugar in a medium bowl and cover with waxed paper. Microwave on high power for 2 minutes. Stir to blend, and serve warm.

STORAGE NOTE: Leftovers can be frozen and used within 1 month or refrigerated and used within 3 days.

Quick-Smoked Baked Beans

I am a huge fan of liquid smoke. If you've never used it, look for it in the condiment and sauce section of the supermarket. It adds the outdoors to your dish, and a little goes a long way.

Yield: 3 servings

1 (16-ounce) can baked beans

1 tablespoon bacon bits

1 tablespoon brown sugar

1 tablespoon ketchup

1 teaspoon liquid smoke

Place the beans, bacon bits, sugar, ketchup, and liquid smoke in a medium bowl and cover with waxed paper. Microwave on high power for 2 minutes. Stir and serve warm.

STORAGE NOTE: Leftovers can be frozen and used within 1 month or refrigerated and used within 3 days.

🕐 *Time-Saving Tip from Tammy*

Brown sugar is simply regular sugar that has had molasses added to make it moist and dark. If you find the pantry bare but need some for a recipe, it's easy to make your own. For light brown sugar, add a tablespoon of molasses or sorghum syrup to a cup of granulated sugar. For dark brown sugar, add 2 tablespoons. Or you can just add the molasses along with the wet ingredients.

Pronto Pimiento Cheese Sandwiches

Pimiento cheese is such a terrific treat for me, but I don't always have time to make it the traditional way. This is my "make-do" sandwich when the craving can't be stopped in spite of a hurried lifestyle. Paprika, which is ground from sweet red peppers, serves as the substitute for pimientos.

Yield: 2 sandwiches

1 heaping cup grated sharp
   cheddar cheese

2 tablespoons mayonnaise

1 teaspoon honey mustard

4 slices white sandwich bread

½ teaspoon paprika

In a small mixing bowl, combine the cheese, mayonnaise, and honey mustard. Spread evenly on two slices of the bread and sprinkle with the paprika. Top with the remaining slices, cut in half on the diagonal, and serve immediately.

STORAGE NOTE: Refrigerate leftovers and use within 5 days.

Elvis's Peanut Butter and Banana Sandwiches

If you've never been to Graceland, it needs to go on your bucket list. There you will discover that the combination of peanut butter and bananas was the King's favorite. While he liked them fried, I prefer just the freshest white bread you've got and cut in half on the diagonal.

Yield: 2 sandwiches

4 slices white bread
½ cup smooth peanut butter

1 banana, peeled and thickly sliced
Potato chips

Place 2 bread slices on each serving plate. Spread 1 slice on each plate with half of the peanut butter. Gently push half of the banana slices into the peanut butter. Top with the remaining bread slices, cut on the diagonal, and serve with potato chips.

BLT PDQ

This is what I used to do in college when I couldn't afford "real" bacon. It is better these days now that the bacon bits are not imitation and come in containers that have larger pieces. A bonus is that the sandwich is simple to slice in half!

Yield: 2 sandwiches

4 slices white sandwich bread

2 tablespoons mayonnaise

2 tablespoons bacon bits

1 small ripe tomato

2 large iceberg lettuce leaves

Place 2 pieces of the bread on serving plates and spread mayonnaise evenly on one side. Sprinkle the bacon bits evenly over the mayonnaise. Slice the tomato and place on top of the bacon bits. Place the lettuce leaves on top of the dry bread slices and top with the remaining half. Cut in half on the diagonal and serve immediately.

Head to the Gazebo Tomato and Basil Sandwiches

This is a classic Southern dish that can easily go from lunch on the gazebo to a Mother's Day celebration when you use large round cookie cutters to remove the bread crust. It's perfect all summer long.

Yield: 4 sandwiches

8 slices fresh white bread

⅓ cup mayonnaise

1 large ripe beefsteak tomato

Kosher salt

Freshly ground black pepper

12 large basil leaves

Spread mayonnaise evenly on the bread slices. Top half of the bread with slices of tomato and sprinkle with salt and pepper. Add 3 basil leaves and top with the remaining bread slices. Cut each sandwich in half horizontally and serve immediately.

Warm Summer Berries and Cream

This recipe is super fast thanks to fresh-picked berries that are already a treat. Slightly warming them accents the flavor and makes them delicious served over ice cream.

Yield: 6 servings

1 pint fresh blueberries

1 pint fresh blackberries

1 pint fresh raspberries

3 tablespoons sugar

Vanilla ice cream

Put the blueberries, blackberries, and raspberries in a large skillet and sprinkle with sugar. Place over high heat and simmer for 2 minutes. Remove from the heat immediately and serve warm over scoops of vanilla ice cream.

STORAGE NOTE: Leftover berries should be covered and refrigerated for use within 2 days. You can freeze the leftovers as well and use within 1 month.

🕐 *Time-Saving Tip from Tammy*

An opened and partially used container of ice cream can form ice crystals on the surface, which can alter the flavor. To prevent this from happening, place a piece of plastic wrap directly over the surface of the ice cream before replacing the cover and returning it to the freezer.

Frosty Frozen Peach Mousse

I use the blender for this dessert, but a food processor will work just as easily. It's perfect for summer dinners on the patio. You'll find peach nectar sold in cans in the fruit juice aisle of the supermarket.

Yield: 8 servings

2 (12-ounce) packages frozen sliced peaches

1 (8-ounce) container plain or vanilla Greek-style yogurt

½ cup powdered sugar

½ cup peach nectar

½ teaspoon pure vanilla or almond extract

1 heaping tablespoon sliced almonds or granola (optional)

Place the peaches in the container of a blender and add the yogurt, sugar, nectar, and extract. Blend until smooth, about 1 minute. Transfer to parfait glasses or short champagne glasses and serve immediately. Top with sliced almonds or granola, if desired.

STORAGE NOTE: This recipe cannot be frozen. You can refrigerate leftovers, but you'll see a bit of thinning occur as the frozen fruit thaws. Stir well before using.

Balsamic Grilled Peaches

Chances are good that your grill will already be in use for dinner when fresh peaches hit the market. Take advantage of that by grilling peach halves just after you pull off the meat. It will give just enough time for the meat to rest. Cover the peaches when done, and when it's time for dessert, drizzle with the vinegar and serve. If little ones are leery of the vinegar, simply omit for their serving.

Yield: 4 servings

4 tablespoons unsalted butter, melted
¼ cup light brown sugar

4 fresh peaches, peeled, halved, and pitted
1 tablespoon aged balsamic vinegar

Preheat the grill to medium. Place the butter in a shallow bowl and the sugar in a separate shallow bowl. Dip the cut end of the peach in the butter, then into the sugar. Arrange with the cut side up on the grate and cook for about 3 minutes. Serve warm drizzled with balsamic vinegar.

STORAGE NOTE: Leftovers can be refrigerated, but should be used within 2 days. Gently reheat in the microwave in 20-second intervals or place back on the grill and heat 1 minute. Do not freeze.

🕐 *Time-Saving Tip from Tammy*

To prevent food from sticking to the grill, make sure you oil it before preheating. There are terrific cooking sprays made for this task or you can dip a paper towel in vegetable oil and rub it on the grate before you begin. Items that usually have the best chance of sticking are those that have been soaking in any type of marinade containing sugar.

Celebration Cherry Sauce

This is a fun dessert sauce to serve in honor of George Washington's birthday. I pour it over slices of toasted pound cake or angel food cake.

Yield: 1 cup

1 (15-ounce) can cherry pie filling   **½ teaspoon sugar**
2 tablespoons maraschino cherry juice

Place the pie filling, juice, and sugar in a blender and puree until smooth. Serve immediately or refrigerate for later use.

Storage Note: Leftovers can be refrigerated and used within 1 week.

Caramel Cream Grapes

Crème fraîche is now available at the supermarket, and I'm so thankful. While it's not difficult to make from scratch, it takes valuable time that I frequently don't have. This recipe is a great one to spotlight cold grapes, tangy crème fraîche, buttery caramel sauce, and crunchy pecans.

Yield: 6 servings

1 cup caramel ice cream topping

3 cups seedless grapes

½ cup crème fraîche or sour cream

Chopped pecans or walnuts

Place the caramel topping in a glass bowl and cover with waxed paper. Microwave 1 minute

In a medium bowl, gently stir together the grapes and crème fraîche. Drizzle the caramel sauce over the grape mixture and sprinkle with the pecans. Serve immediately.

STORAGE NOTE: Leftovers of this recipe can be refrigerated, but you'll see some thinning of the crème fraîche. In addition, the caramel will be cold and the pecans will soften. Use as soon as possible for best quality.

'Cots and Cream

I can find endless uses for canned apricots, and this one is great for steamy summer afternoons. If desired, you can substitute canned peaches.

Yield: 4 servings

1 (14-ounce) can apricot slices
1 tablespoon orange juice
1 tablespoon powdered sugar

1 pint vanilla ice cream
2 tablespoons slivered almonds

Place the apricots and their juice in a blender. Add the orange juice and sugar. Puree until smooth. Spoon over scoops of vanilla ice cream and garnish with the almonds. Serve immediately.

STORAGE NOTE: *The sauce can be refrigerated and used within 5 days. Do not freeze.*

Coconut Snowballs

I love coconut, and this dessert fulfills that craving nicely. It is a 5-minute instant dessert or a 5-minute do-ahead treat. The freezer keeps them ready until you need a coconut fix.

Yield: 5 servings

1 pint coconut or vanilla ice cream   **½ cup shredded coconut**

Roll scoops of ice cream in coconut. Serve immediately.

Storage Note: Wrap each snowball individually in aluminum foil and freeze until needed.

Note: At serving time, top each snowball with a tablespoon of chocolate or caramel syrup, if desired.

Creamy Vanilla Fruit Dip

Vanilla instant pudding mix has come to my rescue numerous times. This dip is great with fresh fruit like strawberries, grapes, sliced bananas, and chunks of cantaloupe, honeydew, and mango.

Yield: 2 ½ cups

1 (3.4-ounce) package vanilla instant pudding mix

2 cups heavy cream

¼ teaspoon pure almond extract

In a mixing bowl, combine the pudding mix, cream, and extract. Set aside to thicken for 3 minutes. Serve with fresh fruit.

Storage Note: Leftovers can be stored in the refrigerator and used within 3 days. Do not freeze.

Pecan-Crusted Strawberries

Easy can still look elegant, and this recipe is the perfect example. What a great ending for any type of meal.

Yield: 4 servings

½ cup sour cream

½ cup packed brown sugar

2 teaspoons powdered sugar

12 fresh strawberries

½ cup crushed nuts (pecan, walnuts, or almonds)

In a small mixing bowl, combine the sour cream, brown sugar, and powdered sugar. Dip strawberries in sour cream mixture, then dredge in the crushed nuts. Serve immediately.

STORAGE NOTE: These can be stored for only the shortest time in the refrigerator. After an hour the nuts soften and the sour cream coating begins slipping.

Chocolate-Drizzled Raspberries

*This is a great-looking dessert that can be prepared at the
last minute or when a sweet-tooth attack happens!*

Yield: 4 to 6 servings

2 ounces milk or dark chocolate   **1 pint fresh raspberries**

8 ounces plain Greek-style yogurt

Place the chocolate in a small glass bowl and microwave on high power for 25 seconds. Stir and, if necessary, heat for another 10 seconds to completely melt.

Meanwhile, pour the yogurt on a serving plate and top with the raspberries. Drizzle the melted chocolate over the top and serve immediately.

STORAGE NOTE: Refrigerate leftovers for 1 day only.

*NOTE: Fresh, capped strawberries can be substituted
for the raspberries if desired.*

Soft-Serve Frozen Fruit Ice Cream

*Use any frozen fruit you want in this recipe, and you've got
a creamy, soft-serve ice cream in only 5 minutes. It's a great
reason to keep frozen fruit on hand all year long!*

Yield: 4 servings

1 (10-ounce) package frozen fruit
(raspberries, blackberries, or
sliced strawberries or peaches)

½ cup sugar

⅔ cup heavy cream

Place the frozen fruit and sugar in the bowl of a food processor or a blender. Process just a few seconds to roughly chop. With the processor or blender running, slowly add the cream until thoroughly mixed. Serve immediately.

STORAGE NOTE: *This recipe can be made ahead and frozen up
to a week, or leftovers can be frozen for up to 1 week.*

🕐 *Time-Saving Tip from Tammy*

Ice cream cones are one of the most beloved instant desserts. Keep those annoying bottom-of-the-cone drips at bay by placing a mini marshmallow in the bottom before filling with scoops. Then it becomes a nice surprise for the last bite when the ice cream is gone.

Marshmallow Fruit Dip

*Marshmallow fluff was a childhood favorite of mine. It is
a great substitute for jelly on peanut butter sandwiches. In
this case, it's paired with fresh fruit for a fun dip.*

Yield: 6 servings

1 (8-ounce) container whipped
   cream cheese

¼ cup marshmallow fluff

3 tablespoons seedless
   raspberry jam or jelly

In a medium mixing bowl, combine the cream cheese, marshmallow fluff, and jam.
Mix until thoroughly blended. Serve immediately with sliced fruit.

Storage Note: Leftovers can be refrigerated and used within 3 days. Do not freeze.

Note: You can substitute strawberry jam or jelly for the raspberry if desired.

Warm Peanut Butter and Chocolate Bananas

*This can be a fun dessert on family movie or game nights
because it hardly takes you away from the action at all!*

Yield: 2 to 4 servings

**2 bananas, peeled and cut
in half lengthwise**

2 tablespoons crunchy peanut butter

**2 tablespoons miniature
semisweet chocolate chips**

Place the bananas with the cut side up on a glass plate. Spread evenly with the peanut butter and sprinkle with the chocolate chips. Microwave on high power for 15 to 20 seconds. Serve immediately.

Mock Blackberry Mojito

*Southerners have been sipping on iced-down fruit drinks for years.
It keeps us cool in the summer and refreshed in the cooler months.
This light but luscious mix is perfect for serving any month. If it's
during the summer, garnish with skewers of fresh blackberries.*

Yield: 7 ½ cups

1 ½ cups blackberry juice blend
   (blackberry-blueberry or
   blackberry-cranberry)

1 (12-ounce) can frozen mojito mix

1 (1-liter) bottle chilled club
   soda or sparkling water

¾ cup ginger ale

1 tablespoon lime juice

In a large pitcher, stir together the blackberry juice, mojito mix, club soda, ginger ale, and lime juice. Serve immediately over ice.

Brunch Butters

There are endless possibilities here, so let your imagination fly! All are right at home served on Old South Buttermilk Biscuits (page 276).

Yield: ½ to ¾ cup

½ cup unsalted butter, softened

Flavor Options:

For Fruit Butter, add 3 tablespoons fruit jam or jelly.

For Nut Butter, add ¼ cup finely chopped toasted walnuts or pecans.

For Syrup Butter, add 3 tablespoons sorghum syrup, honey, or maple syrup.

For Citrus Butter, add 2 teaspoons lemon, lime, or orange juice.

For Citrus-Chile Butter, add 1 tablespoon lime juice, 1 teaspoon lemon juice, 1 teaspoon minced jalapeño peppers, and ½ teaspoon chopped fresh thyme.

For Herb Butter, add 3 teaspoons mixed chopped fresh herbs (chives, parsley, thyme, oregano, or basil in any combination).

For Lemon Herb Butter, make Herb Butter and add 2 teaspoons lemon juice.

For Tarragon Butter, add 2 tablespoons chopped fresh tarragon, 2 tablespoons chopped fresh parsley, 1 teaspoon chopped minced chives, 1 minced garlic clove, and ⅛ teaspoon white pepper.

For Blue Cheese and Pine Nut Butter, add ½ cup crumbled blue cheese, 2 tablespoons pine nuts, and ⅛ teaspoon white pepper.

Place the butter in a small mixing bowl and combine with the flavor option ingredients of your choice. Serve immediately, or cover and chill for later use.

Storage Note: All flavors of butters can be refrigerated and used within 1 week. Do not freeze.

🕐 *Time-Saving Tip from Tammy*

How do you know if butter has come to room temperature when a recipe calls for that? It's ready when the weight of a dinner knife glides through the unwrapped butter with no resistance.

Basil Butter

Lavender Butter

Pecan Butter

Peach Butter

Ginger Nectar Sipper

*Refreshing is how I like to describe this patio drink. It is a great way
to beat the heat while enjoying being out of doors. Canned fruit
nectar is located with the fruit juices at the supermarket.*

Yield: 2 servings

**6 ounces pear, apricot, or
peach nectar, chilled**

**6 ounces ginger ale, chilled
Fresh mint leaves for garnish**

Fill 2 tall glasses with ice and add 3 ounces of the nectar to each glass. Top with the ginger ale and stir. Garnish and serve immediately.

🕐 *Time-Saving Tip from Tammy*

Garnishes for fruit drinks now go well beyond a simple sprig of mint. Fresh fruit that is already a part of the drink makes a beautiful embellishment. If it's berries, just skewer them on a toothpick or wooden skewer and use it as a swizzle stick. If the fruit can be sliced, cut it from one edge to the center and slip it over the glass rim.

Punch Bowl Eggnog without the Punch

Eggnog is such a Southern holiday tradition, and the store-bought versions are quite good. This one is thinned out a bit with milk, making it perfect for the holiday punch bowl.

Yield: 12 servings

½ cup sorghum syrup

2 quarts eggnog

3 cups milk

Grated nutmeg

In a punch bowl, whisk together the sorghum and eggnog until smooth. Add the milk and blend well. Top individual servings with grated nutmeg.

Storage Note: Leftovers can be refrigerated for up to 3 days, but will need significant stirring before serving.

Note: To keep the eggnog cold, place the punch bowl over a larger container of ice.

Cup of Scrambled Eggs with Cheese

*This is a practically instant morning meal when you have to
hit the road fast. Vary the cheese to keep it interesting.*

Yield: 1 serving

2 eggs

2 tablespoons milk

Salt and black pepper to taste

2 tablespoons shredded cheese
(Cheddar, Monterey Jack, or
the cheese of your choice)

Grease a 12-ounce coffee mug with cooking spray and add the eggs, milk, salt, and
pepper. Lightly blend with a fork. Microwave on high power for 45 seconds and stir.
Microwave for 30 to 40 seconds longer or until eggs are almost set. Top with the
cheese and enjoy.

Mock Poinsettia

Champagne is something that is always in my refrigerator, but sometimes you need a nonalcoholic equivalent. This is just as festive and can be enjoyed by everyone in the family. If you have fresh cranberries, skewer a few as a unique swizzle stick.

Yield: 2 servings

16 ounces cranberry juice cocktail, chilled

4 ounces sparkling water or club soda

2 lime wedges

Fill 2 glasses with ice and add equal portions of the cranberry juice. Top with sparkling water and a squeeze of lime, adding the lime wedge to the glass. Stir and serve immediately.

Ready for a Crowd Raspberry Punch

This is a great party punch because it can easily be doubled to fit your needs. With only three ingredients, it is no hassle, as well!

Yield: 12 cups

1 quart raspberry sherbet, softened

1 (12-ounce) can frozen pink lemonade, thawed

1 (2-liter) bottle ginger ale, chilled

In a punch bowl, stir together the sherbet and lemonade until blended. Add the ginger ale and serve immediately.

Perked-Up Cranberry Punch

Pull out the old percolator for this warm holiday drink that will take the chill off.

Yield: 1 gallon

2 (32-ounce) bottles cranberry
juice cocktail

1 (46-ounce) can pineapple juice

2 ½ cups water

1 cup firmly packed dark brown sugar

2 tablespoons whole allspice

2 tablespoons whole cloves

6 (3-inch) sticks cinnamon

Place the cranberry juice, pineapple juice, and water in a large electric percolator. Put the brown sugar, allspice, cloves, and cinnamon in the percolator basket. Perk and serve warm.

Storage Note: Leftovers can be refrigerated and used within 1 week. Gently reheat on the stovetop or in the microwave in 30-second intervals.

Sparkling Fruit Juice

You could serve this juice drink any time of year, but it really sings during the fall and holiday season. Make it a point to keep bottles of club soda in your refrigerator for impromptu get-togethers.

Yield: 6 to 8 servings

2 cups chilled pear nectar

1 cup chilled white grape juice

¼ cup honey

2 (750-milliliter) bottles chilled sparkling apple juice

1 (1-liter) bottle chilled club soda or sparkling water

In a punch bowl or large bowl, whisk together the nectar, grape juice, and honey until smooth. Add the juice and club soda, and mix well. Serve immediately.

Sugared Broiled Grapefruit

*This is one of my favorite ways to begin a cold, winter weekend.
It's like Florida sunshine on a plate and enlivens your taste
buds. And it's a great reason to own grapefruit spoons!*

Yield: 2 servings

1 large grapefruit, halved

4 teaspoons packed dark brown
  sugar, divided

2 teaspoons chopped pecans, divided

Preheat the broiler on high. Place the grapefruit halves on a baking sheet with the cut side up. Sprinkle each half evenly with 2 teaspoons of the brown sugar and 1 teaspoon of the pecans. Broil for 1 to 2 minutes or until the sugar is melted and bubbly. Serve immediately.

🕐 *Time-Saving Tip from Tammy*

Grapefruit spoons have many more uses in the kitchen than just for scooping out the juicy citrus pulp. Use them for cleaning out the seeds of tomatoes, melons, and squash. The serrated edges work in your favor and get the job done efficiently and quickly.

Watermelon Spritzer

Carbonated water turns any fruit juice mixture into a refreshing spritzer. Keep it on hand and in the fridge for quick summer sippers. You can use already cubed fruit that is on sale in the produce department to make this in a snap!

Yield: 6 servings

4 cups cubed seedless watermelon

¾ cup frozen limeade concentrate

4 cups carbonated water

Lime slices for garnish, if desired

Place the watermelon and limeade in a blender. Cover and process until smooth. Transfer to a serving pitcher and add the carbonated water. Garnish and serve immediately.

NOTE: If you prefer a pulp-free drink, process the watermelon and strain in a fine wire mesh sieve. Then add the limeade and stir. Add the carbonated water and serve.

10 Minutes

Cranberry Cheese Spread

Cream cheese is the basic bed for lots of terrific appetizer creations. This one is a great way to kick off the holiday party season. I like to serve it with "everything" crackers.

Yield: 12 servings

2 (8-ounce) packages cream cheese

1 (14-ounce) can cranberry sauce with whole berries

1 (4-ounce) can chopped green chilies, drained

1 green onion, sliced

1 tablespoon lime juice

½ teaspoon seasoned salt

½ teaspoon cayenne pepper

½ teaspoon chili powder

⅛ teaspoon white pepper

Place the cream cheese side by side on a serving plate. In a mixing bowl, combine the cranberry sauce, chilies, onion, lime juice, salt, cayenne, chili powder, and white pepper. Spoon over the cream cheese, allowing it to drip down the sides. Serve with assorted crackers.

STORAGE NOTE: Leftovers can be refrigerated and used within 3 days. Do not freeze.

Smoked Almond Blue Cheese Dip

*Smoked almonds are intensely fabulous, and they add just the
right crunch to this tangy dip that begs for blue corn chips. As
the warm dip cools down, you will find it equally delicious.*

Yield: 2 cups

1 (8-ounce) package cream
   cheese, cut into pieces

1 (4-ounce) package crumbled
   blue cheese

2 garlic cloves, minced

2 tablespoons minced fresh chives

2 tablespoons bacon bits

¼ cup half-and-half

¼ cup chopped smoked almonds

Place the cream cheese, blue cheese, garlic, chives, bacon bits, and half-and-half in
a mixing bowl. Cover with waxed paper and microwave on high power for 1 minute.
Stir and microwave for another minute or until the cheese is completely melted. Stir
to blend and serve warm topped with the smoked almonds.

*STORAGE NOTE: Leftovers should be refrigerated
and used within 3 days. Do not freeze.*

Hummus in a Hurry

Young, tender soybeans are labeled edamame on supermarket shelves. You'll find it already shelled in the produce department, and it's ready to use. It becomes the bean base for this fresh hummus that should be served with nutty sesame or rice crackers.

Yield: 3 cups

1 cup water

1 ½ cups shelled edamame

¼ cup tahini or sesame paste

¼ cup vegetable stock or water

3 tablespoons lemon juice

1 garlic clove, minced

½ teaspoon onion or garlic salt

½ teaspoon ground cumin

¼ teaspoon ground coriander

2 tablespoons olive oil

1 tablespoon chopped fresh parsley

In a heavy saucepan over high heat, bring 1 cup of water and the edamame to a boil. Cook 1 minute. Drain the edamame and set aside to cool. Meanwhile, in a mixing bowl, whisk together the tahini, stock, lemon juice, garlic, salt, cumin, coriander, and oil until smooth. Puree the edamame in the bowl of a food processor until smooth. Stir into the tahini mixture, whisking well. Transfer to a serving bowl and garnish with the parsley.

STORAGE NOTE: Leftovers can be refrigerated and used within 5 days. Do not freeze.

⏱ Time-Saving Tip from Tammy

When you need just a tablespoon or two of sesame paste, don't waste the remaining paste in the container. Remove the paste and transfer it to a small freezer zip-top bag. Press out all the air and flatten the bag, then label and freeze. When you have another recipe that calls for just a bit, you can easily break off the amount you need and return the rest to the freezer. This also works for tomato and garlic paste.

Fire-Roasted Salsa

*The first time I saw canned "fire-roasted" tomatoes in the supermarket,
I was skeptical. Then I conducted a taste test and became a regular
customer. You will too, and this salsa is just the avenue to get you there.*

Yield: 1 ½ cups

1 (14.5-ounce) can fire-roasted
   diced tomatoes, drained

1 small sweet onion, peeled and diced

2 tablespoons chopped fresh cilantro

1 tablespoon lime juice

½ teaspoon sugar

¼ teaspoon garlic salt

⅛ teaspoon white pepper

Place half the tomatoes in a shallow serving bowl, and mash with a potato masher. Stir in the remaining tomatoes, onion, cilantro, lime juice, sugar, garlic salt, and pepper. Serve with tortilla chips.

*STORAGE NOTE: Leftovers can be refrigerated and
used within 5 days. Do not freeze.*

Go Green Hot Ranch Dip

Bring home the fried chicken wings and Buffalo wings, or just pull out fresh celery for this spicy dip. It "goes green" with cilantro, jalapeños, green salsa, and green chilies to give it some kick.

Yield: 2 ¼ cups

1 cup mayonnaise

⅓ cup sour cream

⅓ cup buttermilk

⅓ cup salsa verde

3 tablespoons canned
   chopped green chilies

½ cup fresh cilantro leaves

2 jalapeño peppers, halved and seeded

1 (.4-ounce) package Ranch
   salad dressing mix

Place the mayonnaise, sour cream, buttermilk, salsa, chilies, cilantro, jalapeños, and dressing mix in a blender, and process until smooth. Serve immediately or refrigerate for later use.

STORAGE NOTE: Leftovers can be refrigerated and used within 3 days. Do not freeze.

Kettle Corn

Just a bit of sugar transforms ordinary popped corn into an unexpected treat. The seasonings are in the pan as the corn pops, so all it needs when it's done popping is a drizzle of warm butter.

Yield: 2 to 4 servings

¾ cup popcorn kernels

¼ cup vegetable or canola oil

3 tablespoons sugar

2 teaspoons salt

2 tablespoons unsalted butter, melted

In a large pot with a tight-fitting lid over medium heat, combine the popcorn, oil, sugar, and salt. Shake constantly. When the corn begins to pop, lower the heat slightly to medium-low. Continue to shake until the popping slows. Transfer to a serving bowl and drizzle with melted butter.

STORAGE NOTE: Leftovers should be placed in an airtight container and stored at room temperature.

Goat Cheese and Fig Toasts

There is something refreshing and marvelous about salty goat cheese paired with sweet jam. It satisfies and tingles the taste buds, getting them ready for a great meal. The beauty of this appetizer is that it will hold up, even if guests are running late.

Yield: 12 servings

1 loaf mini-party wheat bread, sliced

1 (8-ounce) log plain goat cheese

1 (6-ounce) jar fig jam

Fresh thyme for garnish

Preheat the broiler on high, and arrange the bread in a single layer on the broiler rack. Broil for 1 to 2 minutes or until the bread slices are lightly browned. Smear each slice with about a tablespoon of the goat cheese and transfer to a serving plate. Place a teaspoon-size dollop of jam on the top of each toast, garnish with fresh thyme, and serve.

STORAGE NOTE: *Refrigerate leftovers and use within 1 day.*

🕐 *Time-Saving Tip from Tammy*

Those handy rubber gloves that we all have for hot water dishwashing are also great for opening those hard to twist jars that seem to have lids permanently attached.

Pecan and Parmesan Crusted Brie

I had this crusty-on-the-outside, creamy-on-the-inside cheese at a dinner party and begged for the recipe. It is divine and my favorite way to serve Brie.

Yield: 8 servings

¼ cup vegetable oil

1 egg

¼ cup seasoned dry breadcrumbs

¼ cup ground pecans

¼ cup grated Parmesan cheese

1 (8-ounce) round Brie cheese

Put the oil in a medium skillet and place over medium heat. Meanwhile, in a shallow round dish, beat the egg. In a separate shallow round dish, combine the breadcrumbs, pecans, and Parmesan. Dip the Brie in the egg to coat the top and bottom rinds, then dip in the breadcrumb mixture. Repeat, and then place in the hot oil. Brown for 2 minutes on each side and serve warm.

STORAGE NOTE: Leftovers should be refrigerated and used within 1 week. Gently reheat in the microwave at 20-second intervals. Do not freeze.

Shrimp and Green Olive Spread

*The little flecks of green and red in this spread add to the
festive appeal. I usually serve it slightly warm, but it can be
covered and refrigerated, then served cold if you wish.*

Yield: 1 3/4 cups

1 (8-ounce) package cream
    cheese, softened

6 pimiento-stuffed green
    olives, chopped

2 tablespoons mayonnaise

2 tablespoons minced shallots

1 teaspoon lemon juice

¼ teaspoon Worcestershire sauce

¼ teaspoon hot sauce

⅛ teaspoon garlic powder

⅛ teaspoon white pepper

½ pound salad shrimp, coarsely chopped

Place the cream cheese, olives, mayonnaise, shallots, lemon juice, Worcestershire
sauce, hot sauce, garlic powder, and pepper in a glass mixing bowl. Microwave on
high power for 30 to 45 seconds. Stir in the shrimp and serve with assorted crackers.

*STORAGE NOTE: Leftovers should be refrigerated
and used within 3 days. Do not freeze.*

⏱ *Time-Saving Tip from Tammy*

When wooden cutting boards start looking dry, give them a light coat of food-grade
mineral oil applied with a paper towel. It
will revive the wood and lengthen the life
of your cutting board. Do not wash the oil
application off. Allow it to penetrate the
wood and rehydrate it.

Watermelon and Cantaloupe Salsa

*During the summer fruit season, you may tend to have containers of
assorted leftovers in the fridge. This recipe makes use of those bowls
of watermelon and cantaloupe in a zesty salsa that's terrific with blue
corn chips. It's also a good garnish on grilled seafood or chicken.*

Yield: 4 cups

1 pound watermelon, cut in ¼-inch dice

1 pound cantaloupe, cut into ¼-inch dice

½ red bell pepper, chopped

1 shallot, peeled and chopped

1 small jalapeño pepper, finely chopped

¼ cup chopped fresh cilantro

1 tablespoon lime juice

¼ teaspoon salt

In a mixing bowl, combine the watermelon, cantaloupe, red bell pepper, shallot,
jalapeño pepper, cilantro, lime juice, and salt. Toss gently, and serve with chips

*STORAGE NOTE: Leftovers should be refrigerated
and used within 1 week. Do not freeze.*

Walnut and Pear Preserve Wedges

This unique use of ordinary tortillas marries the harvests of a Southern fall. Crunchy walnuts, chunky pear preserves, and creamy Havarti cheese make this appetizer a terrific hit to start off your dinner party.

Yield: 3 to 4 appetizer servings

2 (10-inch) whole wheat or flour tortillas

½ cup shredded Havarti cheese

2 heaping tablespoons chopped walnuts

½ cup pear preserves

Place 1 tortilla in a lightly greased skillet over medium-high heat. Sprinkle the cheese and walnuts evenly over the top. Cover with the other tortilla and cook for 2 minutes, then flip and cook for 2 minutes longer. Transfer to a serving plate, and cut into wedges with a pizza cutter. Serve immediately with the pear preserves.

STORAGE NOTE: Leftovers should be refrigerated and used within 3 days. Gently reheat in the microwave in 15-second intervals. Do not freeze.

Autumn Garden Salad

This salad should be pulled together just before serving, which keeps the pear slices from oxidizing and turning brown. If you don't have any pears, feel free to substitute apples.

Yield: 6 servings

1 (6-ounce) package fresh mesclun mix

1 pear, sliced

¼ cup chopped walnuts

¼ cup dried cherries

¼ cup vegetable oil

2 tablespoons apple cider vinegar

2 tablespoons sugar

¼ teaspoon salt

⅛ teaspoon black pepper

Place the greens, pear, walnuts, and cherries in a salad bowl, and toss. In a jar with a tight-fitting lid, combine the oil, vinegar, sugar, salt, and pepper. Shake to emulsify. Pour over the salad, toss, and serve immediately.

Storage Note: Leftovers should be refrigerated and used within 1 day.

Country Ham and Peach Salad

*I love mixtures of salty and sweet. This salad hits the mark for both
and can transition from a light lunch to an elegant dinner.*

Yield: 4 servings

2 tablespoons olive oil

2 tablespoons lemon juice

2 teaspoons honey

¼ teaspoon black pepper

⅛ teaspoon salt

1 (6.5-ounce) package butter lettuce

2 peaches, peeled and cut into slices

⅓ cup shaved country ham
   (or finely diced)

⅓ cup crumbled goat cheese

2 tablespoons sunflower seeds

In a jar with a tight-fitting lid, combine the oil, juice, honey, pepper, and salt. Shake to emulsify. Divide the lettuce among 4 salad plates. Top evenly with the peaches, ham, and goat cheese. Drizzle the dressing over the top, and sprinkle evenly with the sunflower seeds. Serve immediately.

STORAGE NOTE: Leftovers should be refrigerated and used within 1 day.

Crunchy Broccoli Salad

If you aren't a fan of bacon, don't skip over this recipe. Simply substitute soy bits, and you've still got a great side salad.

Yield: 4 to 6 servings

4 cups chopped broccoli florets

2 Roma tomatoes, chopped

1 cup sliced mushrooms

4 tablespoons mayonnaise

2 tablespoons milk

1 teaspoon dried parsley

½ teaspoon garlic powder

¼ teaspoon white pepper

2 tablespoons crunchy bacon bits
   (not ground, but large pieces)

Place the broccoli, tomatoes, and mushrooms in a serving bowl. In a small mixing bowl, whisk together the mayonnaise, milk, parsley, garlic powder, and white pepper. Gently toss over the broccoli mixture to evenly coat. Sprinkle with the bacon bits and serve immediately.

STORAGE NOTE: Leftovers should be refrigerated and used within 3 days. Do not freeze.

🕐 *Time-Saving Tip from Tammy*

Don't limit your egg slicer to just eggs. It's also great for producing even slices of fresh mushrooms and cored, capped strawberries.

Hasty Tasty Seafood Potato Soup

Enhancing canned cream soup with just the right mixture of colorful ingredients makes this soup seem like a more complicated culinary concoction. The tiny salad shrimp are just the right size to fit on the spoon!

Yield: 6 servings

1 (10.75-ounce) can cream
   of potato soup

1 (14.75-ounce) can chicken stock

2 cups milk

½ cup chopped green onions

1 (6.5-ounce) can small salad
   shrimp or crabmeat, drained

¼ teaspoon black pepper

Seasoned croutons for garnish

Paprika for garnish

Place the potato soup, stock, and milk in a large saucepan over high heat. Add the onions, shrimp, and pepper to the soup mixture. Heat and stir frequently for 7 minutes or until just starting to boil. Serve warm with a garnish of croutons and a sprinkling of paprika.

STORAGE NOTE: Leftovers should be refrigerated and used within 3 days. Do not freeze.

🕐 *Time-Saving Tip from Tammy*

A large pot with a pasta insert is the handiest tool you've got in your kitchen when making homemade stock. Just lift the insert out when sufficiently cooked and there's no mess or splatter from trying to pour the solids through a strainer.

Pecan Greens with Cumin-Mustard Vinaigrette

Dressings that are homemade are phenomenal. This is one of my favorites because it's so different from any bottled dressing I've ever tasted. You'll find lots of reasons to whisk it together. Add leftover diced cooked chicken, turkey, or ham to your salad and you've got a complete meal.

Yield: 4 to 6 servings

6 cups mixed salad greens

1 cup chopped pecans

½ cup olive oil

3 tablespoons white wine vinegar

2 tablespoons Dijon mustard

¼ teaspoon ground cumin

¼ teaspoon salt

¼ teaspoon sugar

⅛ teaspoon black pepper

Place the greens in a serving bowl and sprinkle with the pecans. In a jar with a tight-fitting lid, combine the oil, vinegar, mustard, cumin, salt, sugar, and pepper. Shake well to emulsify, and pour over the greens. Toss gently and serve.

STORAGE NOTE: Leftovers should be refrigerated and used within 1 day.

Nutty Cranberry Spinach Salad

*I enjoyed a version of this salad at a restaurant and immediately
tried to duplicate it at home. I love toasted pine nuts, and this
salad should be a reason to keep them on hand at all times.*

Yield: 4 servings

¼ cup pine nuts

4 cups baby spinach leaves

¼ cup dried cranberries

¼ cup rice vinegar

¼ cup sesame or peanut oil

¼ cup light brown sugar

1 tablespoon soy sauce

2 teaspoons dried onion flakes

½ teaspoon curry powder

¼ teaspoon salt

⅛ teaspoon white pepper

Preheat the oven to 350°F. Place the pine nuts in a single layer on a baking sheet and put them in the oven before it finishes preheating. Toast for 5 minutes.

Meanwhile, place the spinach leaves in a serving bowl, and toss with the cranberries. In a jar with a tight-fitting lid, combine the vinegar, oil, sugar, soy sauce, onion flakes, curry powder, salt, and pepper. Shake to emulsify. Drizzle over the salad, and toss with the warm pine nuts just before serving.

STORAGE NOTE: Leftovers should be refrigerated and used within 1 day.

Pecan, Pear, and Gorgonzola Salad

Color is the key to making a salad appetizing to the eyes. This one mixes bright pears with crisp mixed spring greens. The blast of red from radicchio in the mix gets your mouth ready for the tangy raspberry vinaigrette.

Yield: 8 servings

1 cup chopped pecans or walnuts

2 large pears, cored and sliced thin

1 tablespoon lemon juice

6 cups mixed spring greens

1 (4-ounce) container crumbled Gorgonzola cheese

½ cup Raspberry Dressing (page 18)

Preheat the oven to 350°F. Spread the chopped nuts on a baking pan and place in the oven while it finishes preheating. Toast for a total of 4 minutes or until fragrant and golden brown.

Meanwhile, toss the sliced pears with lemon juice to prevent discoloration. Place the greens in a serving bowl, and toss with the cheese and vinaigrette. Add the pears and warm pecans. Toss and serve immediately.

STORAGE NOTE: Leftovers should be refrigerated and used within 1 day for best quality.

In a Pinch Pea Soup

*Everyone has had company drop by unexpectedly and had that
panicked moment when you wonder what you will serve for lunch
or dinner. Head to the pantry because this is your solution!*

Yield: 6 servings

2 (10.75-ounce) cans consommé*

2 (14.75-ounce) cans field
   peas, undrained

1 teaspoon ketchup

¼ teaspoon onion or garlic powder

¼ teaspoon black pepper

2 tablespoons water

Chopped fresh chives for garnish

Place the consommé, peas, ketchup, onion powder, and pepper in a large saucepan
over high heat. Stir and cook for 5 minutes. Stir in the water and heat for 2 to 3 minutes
longer. Serve warm with a garnish of chopped fresh chives.

*STORAGE NOTE: Leftovers should be refrigerated and used
within 4 days. Freeze for no more than 2 months.*

*You absolutely must use consommé in this recipe. Beef broth will not work.

Ranch Beans

These quick beans are great served with hamburgers or hot dogs from the grill, and you don't have to miss the party getting them ready.

Yield: 6 servings

1 (16-ounce) can baked beans

1 (15.5-ounce) can red kidney beans, drained

¼ cup finely chopped green bell pepper

2 tablespoons ketchup

2 tablespoons sorghum or maple syrup

1 tablespoon light brown sugar

1 tablespoon Dijon mustard

½ teaspoon dried onions

Place the baked beans, kidney beans, bell pepper, ketchup, sorghum, sugar, mustard, and onions in a glass bowl. Mix well and cover with waxed paper. Microwave on high power for 5 minutes, stirring halfway through. Serve warm.

STORAGE NOTE: Leftovers should be refrigerated and used within 4 days. They can also be frozen but should be used within 1 month.

Broiled Parmesan Garden Tomatoes

This recipe would make even winter tomatoes taste good. But nothing matches the flavor of those right off the vine. Serve it with grilled fish or chicken.

Yield: 4 servings

2 large tomatoes, cut in half

4 tablespoons unsalted butter, divided

4 green onions, chopped

3 tablespoons dry seasoned
   breadcrumbs

1 ½ tablespoons grated
   Parmesan cheese

¼ cup shredded Monterey
   Jack or Swiss cheese

Preheat the broiler on high. Place the tomatoes with the cut side up on an ungreased broiler rack, and dot evenly with 2 tablespoons of butter. Broil 6 inches from the heat source for 4 minutes.

Meanwhile, combine the remaining butter and onions in a glass bowl and microwave on high power uncovered for 2 minutes. Stir in the breadcrumbs and Parmesan. Spoon on top of the tomatoes and sprinkle with the Monterey Jack cheese. Broil 1 minute longer and serve hot.

STORAGE NOTE: Leftovers should be chopped and stored in the refrigerator. Use within 3 days as a pasta or salad topping.

Carrots and Peas, Please

This combination of sweet early vegetables has been around a long time, and it never gets old. I love that it adds a punch of vibrant color to any plate and pairs with practically any meat. It's the ideal side dish for dinner.

Yield: 4 servings

½ cup water

1 ¼ cups baby carrot slices

2 cups frozen English peas

2 tablespoons unsalted butter, softened

2 teaspoons dried onions

¼ teaspoon dried thyme

⅛ teaspoon sugar

⅛ teaspoon black pepper

Place ½ cup of water in a saucepan over high heat and add the carrots. Cover and cook for 3 minutes. Remove the lid, add the peas, and cook 1 minute more. Drain and stir in the butter, onions, thyme, sugar, and pepper. Stir until the butter melts, and serve hot.

STORAGE NOTE: Leftovers should be refrigerated and used within 4 days. Do not freeze.

Walnut Broccoli

This side dish is versatile and beautiful. I love the nutty crunch the walnuts add to this dish, and the cheese holds it all together nicely.

Yield: 4 servings

1 (16-ounce) package frozen chopped broccoli, thawed
½ cup chopped walnuts
4 tablespoons unsalted butter

¼ teaspoon onion or garlic salt
¼ teaspoon black pepper
½ cup shredded Swiss cheese

Place the broccoli and walnuts in a glass bowl. Dot with the butter and sprinkle with the salt and pepper. Cover with waxed paper and microwave on high power for 3 minutes. Top with the cheese and microwave 1 minute longer. Serve immediately.

STORAGE NOTE: Leftovers should be refrigerated and used within 2 days. Do not freeze.

Jicama and Red Cabbage Slaw

This vibrant coleslaw makes your ordinary fish dinner come alive. You'll find it changes flavor the longer it sits. Utilize a food processor to speed the process along.

Yield: 8 to 10 servings

2 cups thinly sliced jicama (about half a medium-size jicama)

2 cups shredded red cabbage (about half a medium head)

¼ cup thinly sliced sweet onions

¼ cup chopped fresh cilantro

2 tablespoons olive oil

2 tablespoons lime juice

½ teaspoon salt

½ teaspoon sugar

¼ teaspoon white pepper

In a large bowl, combine the jicama, cabbage, onions, and cilantro. In a jar with a tight-fitting lid, combine the oil, juice, salt, sugar, and pepper, and shake to emulsify. Pour over the vegetables, and toss to evenly coat. Serve at room temperature or cold.

STORAGE NOTE: Leftovers should be refrigerated and used within 4 days. Do not freeze.

Spice of Life Vegetables

This colorful combination of vegetables makes it a natural for serving with grilled fish or roasted chicken. I like it served at room temperature, but you can mix it together ahead of time and serve it cold if you like.

Yield: 6 servings

1 (16-ounce) can stewed tomatoes

1 (8.75-ounce) can whole kernel corn, drained

1 cup chopped cucumber

2 garlic cloves, minced

2 tablespoons chopped orange bell pepper

2 tablespoons chopped green onions, green parts only

2 tablespoons red wine vinegar

½ teaspoon ground cumin

¼ teaspoon dried cilantro

¼ teaspoon seasoned salt

¼ teaspoon white pepper

Place the tomatoes, corn, cucumber, garlic, bell pepper, onions, vinegar, cumin, cilantro, salt, and pepper in a serving bowl. Toss gently and serve.

STORAGE NOTE: *Leftovers should be refrigerated and used within 4 days. Do not freeze.*

🕐 *Time-Saving Tip from Tammy*

Onions and bell peppers are the only two vegetables that do not require blanching before freezing. When you see these items on sale at the supermarket, stock up. Then just peel the onions and chop, and seed the peppers and chop. They can go straight into a heavy-duty freezer bag that has been labeled, and you've got these two staples whenever you need them. Bonus: No need to thaw ahead of time; just break off the amount you need and throw it into your simmering soup, stew, or casserole.

Raw Tomato Compote

Think outside the box with this recipe. This is not salsa. It's a saucy side dish for practically any grilled or pan-fried meat from fish to chicken-fried steak. Spoon it on the top of the entrée, and let it spill generously onto the side. It's also terrific with grilled whole artichokes.

Yield: 3 servings

6 plum or Roma tomatoes, seeded and coarsely chopped

2 green onions, finely chopped

½ cup coarsely chopped fresh basil

1 garlic clove, minced

2 teaspoons olive oil

2 teaspoons sugar

¼ cup white wine or champagne vinegar

½ teaspoon seasoned salt

In a serving bowl, combine the tomatoes, green onions, and basil. In a jar with a tight-fitting lid, combine the garlic, olive oil, sugar, vinegar, and salt. Shake to emulsify, and pour over the tomato mixture. Toss and serve.

STORAGE NOTE: This compote can be covered and refrigerated up to 3 days. Do not freeze.

Smashed Pinto Beans

*Pinto beans are traditionally served with freshly baked wedges
of hot corn bread, but who has time to soak and cook beans all
day? This healthy recipe uses canned beans that are pureed. It is
a great side dish or can substitute as a spread for wraps.*

Yield: 4 servings

1 (15.75-ounce) can pinto beans, drained   **½ cup salsa**
1 green onion, sliced   **¼ teaspoon cayenne**

Place the beans in the bowl of a food processor, and puree until smooth. Transfer to a glass bowl, and stir in the onions, salsa, and cayenne. Cover with waxed paper and heat in the microwave on high power for 3 minutes. Serve warm.

*Storage Note: Leftovers can be refrigerated and used
within 4 days or frozen and used within 1 month.*

Sautéed Wild Mushrooms

If you can find morels for this dish, grab them! Their smoky,
nutty flavor seems to come alive when quickly sautéed. However,
any wild mushroom will work, including an assortment.

Yield: 4 servings

1 tablespoon unsalted butter

1 garlic clove, minced

½ pound wild mushrooms

¼ cup chicken stock

½ teaspoon sea salt

¼ teaspoon black pepper

In a large skillet over medium heat, melt the butter. Add the garlic and cook 1 minute. Stir in the mushrooms and cook, stirring gently for 3 minutes. Add the stock and cook for 2 minutes more. Season with the salt and pepper and serve warm.

STORAGE NOTE: Leftovers should be refrigerated
and used within 4 days. Do not freeze.

⏲ *Time-Saving Tip from Tammy*

Fresh mushrooms act like little sponges, and washing them with water can cause them to become waterlogged. A better way to "wash" them is to brush them with a vegetable brush that contains soft bristles and can get under the gills to remove even stubborn dirt. If you don't have one, an inexpensive alternative is to use a new soft-bristled toothbrush.

Squash, Baby

You could spend time and money searching out baby squash varieties on the market, or you can simply harvest them while still small from your garden. Or ask your local supplier to do it for you from their own supplies. Either way, you've got a side dish that sings in a matter of minutes.

Yield: 6 servings

2 tablespoons vegetable oil

1 pound baby yellow squash,
  halved lengthwise

½ pound baby zucchini,
  halved lengthwise

1 cup chopped leeks

½ teaspoon salt

¼ teaspoon black pepper

½ cup crumbled Feta cheese

2 tablespoons finely chopped
  fresh basil or parsley

Heat the oil in a large skillet over medium-high heat. Add the yellow squash, zucchini, and leeks. Sauté for 5 minutes or until tender. Season with the salt and pepper. Sprinkle with the cheese and basil, and serve warm.

STORAGE NOTE: Leftovers should be refrigerated and used within 4 days. Do not freeze.

Fresh Spinach Sauté

Packaged fresh spinach is a supreme time saver. Instead of standing at the sink washing bunches, you've got the side dish made and ready to brighten a plate. This recipe is excellent served with grilled meat or roasted pork.

Yield: 2 servings

2 tablespoons canola oil

2 garlic cloves, minced

1 (6-ounce) package fresh baby spinach

¼ cup slivered almonds

⅛ teaspoon cayenne

Place the oil in a large skillet over medium-high heat. Add the garlic, and sauté 1 minute. Add the spinach and almonds, and sauté for 4 minutes longer. Stir in the cayenne. Serve hot.

STORAGE NOTE: Leftovers should be refrigerated and used within 2 days. Do not freeze.

Squash Toothpicks

Use any type of summer squash in this recipe, and you'll love the results. The yellow squash can be straight or crookneck, and pattypan makes a great substitution for the zucchini.

Yield: 4 to 6 servings

¼ cup vegetable stock or water

1 tablespoon unsalted butter

2 yellow squash, trimmed

2 zucchini, trimmed

½ teaspoon salt

¼ teaspoon white pepper

In a medium saucepan over high heat, bring the stock and butter to a boil. Meanwhile, either by hand or in a food processor, grate the squash and zucchini. Add the squash to the boiling stock, and reduce the heat to medium-low. Cook and stir for 3 minutes. Season with the salt and pepper, and serve immediately.

STORAGE NOTE: Leftovers should be refrigerated and served within 4 days. Do not freeze.

Steamed and Buttered Florets

This could become the recipe you pull out on a weekly basis. I use it to empty bits and pieces of leftover items in my vegetable bin. If you are in a real hurry, pick up broccoli and cauliflower florets from the salad bar at your local supermarket.

Yield: 2 servings

1 cup broccoli florets

½ cup cauliflower florets

2 tablespoons chopped fresh parsley, chives, tarragon, or basil

¼ teaspoon salt

¼ teaspoon white pepper

2 tablespoons unsalted butter, cut into pieces

Arrange the broccoli and cauliflower on a glass plate with the cauliflower toward the outside. Sprinkle the herbs, salt, and pepper over the top, and dot with the butter. Cover tightly with plastic wrap, and cook in the microwave on high power for 5 minutes. Uncover, toss, and serve warm.

Storage Note: Leftovers should be refrigerated and used within 2 days. Do not freeze.

Note: You can substitute green beans, peas, red cabbage, or sugar snap peas for the broccoli or cauliflower if desired.

Lemon Buttered Carrots

I love carrots prepared any way, but this one is great with beef. The carrots are cooked, but still crunchy, and I love the tang that lemon adds to the buttery mix.

Yield: 4 servings

1 pound fresh baby carrots

2 tablespoons water

2 tablespoons unsalted butter

1 tablespoon lemon juice

½ teaspoon grated lemon zest

¼ teaspoon salt

⅛ teaspoon black pepper

Place the carrots and water in a glass bowl, cover with waxed paper, and microwave on high power for 5 minutes. Meanwhile, in a separate small glass bowl, combine the butter, lemon juice, zest, salt, and pepper. When the carrots have finished cooking, remove from the microwave, but leave covered. Microwave the butter mixture for 20 seconds or until the butter is melted. Drain the carrots and pour the butter mixture over, tossing to evenly coat. Serve hot.

STORAGE NOTE: Leftovers should be refrigerated and used within 4 days. Do not freeze.

Apple, Peanut Butter, and Bacon Sandwiches

This unlikely combination is quite honestly the most addictive sandwich you can make on the fly.

Yield: 2 sandwiches

6 bacon slices

4 slices whole-wheat bread, lightly toasted

½ cup creamy peanut butter

1 small apple, cored and thinly sliced

Place the bacon in a single layer on a plate and cover with waxed paper. Microwave on high power for 3 minutes or until crispy. Meanwhile, lightly toast the bread in a toaster. Place 2 slices of bread on each serving plate and evenly spread the peanut butter on all 4 pieces. Add the apple slices, slightly pressing into the peanut butter. Drain the bacon on paper towels and add 3 slices to each sandwich. Place the slices together and cut in half. Serve immediately.

Eat the Heat Turkey Cheese Chili

Canned chili is a real time saver during the colder months when we need warming up from the inside out. This recipe uses turkey chili that is accessorized with additional vegetables and cheese.

Yield: 6 servings

2 (15-ounce) cans turkey chili with beans

1 (11-ounce) can white shoepeg corn, drained

2 Roma tomatoes, chopped

¼ cup chopped green onions

½ teaspoon cayenne

½ cup cubed Mexican processed cheese product (such as Mexican-flavored Velveeta)

2 tablespoons chopped fresh parsley

Place the chili, corn, tomatoes, green onions, and cayenne in a large glass bowl and cover with waxed paper. Microwave on high power for 2 minutes while you cube the cheese and chop the parsley. Stir the mixture well and add the cheese. Recover and microwave on high power for 2 minutes or until the cheese has completely melted. Stir again and ladle into serving bowls. Garnish with the parsley, and serve immediately.

STORAGE NOTE: Leftovers should be refrigerated and used within 4 days. Do not freeze.

🕐 *Time-Saving Tip from Tammy*

Microwave ovens can get dirty quickly when items are not covered before cooking. To clean the mess, place a large bowl of water in the microwave and cook on high power for 10 minutes. The steaming action will loosen stuck-on food particles that can then be wiped away easily.

Cajun Shrimp and Rice

Ready-to-serve rice is a great item to grab when you are in a rush to get something substantial on the table. In this case, it is embellished with delicious spiced shrimp and crunchy snow peas.

Yield: 4 servings

1 (8.8-ounce) package
   ready-to-serve rice

2 teaspoons Cajun seasoning

1 tablespoon canola oil

1 tablespoon unsalted butter

1 pound medium shrimp,
   peeled and deveined

1 (6-ounce) package frozen
   snow peas, thawed

1 large garlic clove, minced

Cook the rice in the microwave according to the package directions. Meanwhile, place the Cajun seasoning, oil, and butter in a large skillet over medium-high heat. Add the shrimp, snow peas, and garlic, and cook for 4 minutes or until the shrimp are just done and pink.

Transfer the rice to a serving bowl, and top with the shrimp mixture. Serve immediately.

STORAGE NOTE: Leftovers should be refrigerated and used within 4 days. Do not freeze.

Grilled Cheese and Bacon on Raisin Bread

I know what you are thinking, but you cannot believe how delicious this combination is. I had it at a neighborhood deli and have been making it at home ever since. Give it a try!

Yield: 2 sandwiches

6 bacon slices

4 slices raisin bread

1 tablespoon unsalted butter

¼ pound thinly sliced extra-sharp Cheddar cheese

Place the bacon in a single layer on a plate and cover with waxed paper. Microwave on high power for 3 minutes or until crispy. Meanwhile, spread the raisin bread slices evenly with the butter. Place a large nonstick skillet over medium heat until hot. Add 2 slices of the raisin bread with the buttered side down. Top evenly with the cheese slices and bacon. Top with the remaining bread, leaving the buttered side up.

Grill 1 minute on each side, pressing lightly with a spatula. The sandwiches are ready when the cheese is melted and the bread is golden brown. Serve warm.

Mustard-Smeared Fish Fillets

I have been using mustard or mayonnaise to glaze and moisten fish for years. In this case, I like the combination of the two. Use tilapia, catfish, halibut, perch, or orange roughy fillets.

Yield: 4 servings

4 (6-ounce) fish fillets

¼ cup mayonnaise

3 tablespoons yellow mustard

1 tablespoon lemon juice

1 tablespoon horseradish

Cracked black pepper

Preheat the broiler on high, and lightly grease a broiler pan with cooking spray. Arrange the fish with the flat side up on the rack, and broil 6 inches from the heat source for 2 minutes. Meanwhile, in a small mixing bowl, combine the mayonnaise, mustard, juice, and horseradish.

Carefully turn the fish and spoon the sauce mixture evenly on the top. Broil for 4 minutes longer or until the fish flakes easily with a fork. Crack black pepper to taste over the top, and serve immediately.

STORAGE NOTE: Leftovers should be refrigerated and used within 2 days. Do not freeze.

Pecan Pimiento Cheese

I consider myself a pimiento cheese expert. I love it cold smeared on fresh white bread or grilled and served warm. This recipe can go both ways and lasts for up to a week in the refrigerator.

Yield: 6 to 8 servings

1 ¼ cups mayonnaise

1 (4-ounce) jar diced pimientos, drained

1 teaspoon Worcestershire sauce

1 teaspoon finely grated onions

¼ teaspoon cayenne pepper

¼ teaspoon sugar

1 (16-ounce) package shredded sharp Cheddar cheese

¼ cup chopped pecans

2 tablespoons chopped fresh parsley

Stir together the mayonnaise, pimientos, Worcestershire sauce, onions, cayenne, and sugar. Add the cheese, pecans, and parsley. Stir gently to evenly coat. Serve immediately.

STORAGE NOTE: Leftovers should be refrigerated and used within 1 week.

Smoked Salmon Egg Salad

*When I am in the kitchen doing other things, I put some eggs on
the stove to boil and have them ready for adding to green salads,
deviling, or using in this great recipe. Serve it over mixed greens, or
put it between thick slices of toasted bread for a hearty lunch.*

Yield: 6 servings

5 hard-cooked eggs, chopped

1 (4.5-ounce) package smoked
   salmon, chopped

2 green onions, chopped

½ cup mayonnaise

¼ cup sour cream

1 teaspoon dried dill

½ teaspoon lemon juice

¼ teaspoon garlic salt

⅛ teaspoon black pepper

In a serving bowl, combine the eggs, salmon, onions, mayonnaise, sour cream, dill,
lemon juice, garlic salt, and pepper. Mix well and serve.

*STORAGE NOTE: Leftovers should be refrigerated
and used within 2 days. Do not freeze.*

Spicy Chicken Tenders

I love odd spice combinations, and this one uses some that you probably don't frequently pull from the spice rack. This can be served with steamed vegetables or a green salad.

Yield: 4 servings

1 pound chicken tenders

2 tablespoons water

½ teaspoon crushed red pepper

½ teaspoon curry powder

½ teaspoon salt

¼ teaspoon paprika

¼ teaspoon ground turmeric

¼ teaspoon ground ginger

⅛ teaspoon white pepper

Preheat the broiler on high, and lightly grease a broiler pan with cooking spray. Place the chicken tenders on the pan and set aside.

In a small mixing bowl, combine the water, crushed red pepper, curry powder, salt, paprika, turmeric, ginger, and white pepper. Brush the spice mixture on both sides of the tenders. Broil 6 inches from the heat source for 3 minutes on each side or until the chicken is no longer pink. Serve hot.

STORAGE NOTE: Leftovers should be refrigerated and used within 4 days. Or they can be frozen and used within 2 months.

Fruit Kabobs with Hot Fudge Sauce

*Sometimes simple is best. These fruit kabobs can change as the
fruit season shifts from berries to stone fruits to melons. You can
substitute caramel or butterscotch sauce for the fudge if desired.*

Yield: 6 servings

1 (15-ounce) jar hot fudge sauce

1 firm banana, peeled and
   cut into ½-inch slices

12 large marshmallows, cut in half

24 medium strawberries

Place the hot fudge sauce in a glass bowl and microwave on medium power for 2
minutes. Meanwhile, alternate the banana slices, marshmallows, and strawberries
on 6 wooden skewers. Place on a serving plate.

Stir the hot fudge sauce and heat another minute. Serve the warm sauce with the
fruit kabobs.

*STORAGE NOTE: Leftovers should be refrigerated and used
within 2 days for best quality. Gently reheat the sauce in the
microwave in 15-second intervals. Do not freeze.*

Caramel Fondue

*Simple apple wedges have never tasted as good as they will when
dipped in this luxurious sauce. Save any leftovers to drizzle over
the top of warm apple pie or scoops of vanilla ice cream.*

Yield: 3 servings

⅔ cup heavy cream   **10 individual caramel candies**

In a small saucepan over medium heat, combine the cream and the caramels. Cook,
stirring constantly, for 5 to 6 minutes or until the caramels melt. Serve warm.

*STORAGE NOTE: Leftovers should be refrigerated and used within 4 days.
Gently reheat in the microwave in 15-second intervals. Do not freeze.*

*NOTE: If desired, add ¼ cup of toasted chopped
pecans or walnuts to the mixture.*

🕐 *Time-Saving Tip from Tammy*

Leftover fondue becomes remarkably firm
after it cools down. In order to reheat it with
the freshest-tasting results, nestle a micro-
wavable bowl containing the leftover fondue
in a slightly larger bowl that has been filled
about one-third with water. Microwave the
set on high power for 2 minutes and serve
immediately.

Cherry Clouds

In a pinch, you get creative. A friend of mine found herself in such a spot with unexpected guests. This came to her rescue, and I've used it numerous times as well. It's equally delicious layered in parfait glasses.

Yield: 4 servings

4 ounces cream cheese

½ cup frozen whipped topping, thawed

4 chocolate sandwich cookies, crushed

1 cup cherry pie filling

Place the cream cheese in a medium glass bowl, and microwave on high power for 15 seconds. Whisk in the whipped topping and blend well. Spoon onto four dessert plates, and use the back of a spoon to create a cavity in the center.

Sprinkle the inside of the "shells" with the cookie crumbs, then top with ¼ cup of the pie filling. Serve immediately.

Cherry and Hazelnut Delight

*This dessert is a delight in every bite. It's a great,
simple dessert that looks a little fancy.*

Yield: 4 servings

4 tablespoons shredded coconut

1 (21-ounce) can cherry pie filling

**1 (8-ounce) container frozen
whipped topping, thawed**

1 cup chopped hazelnuts

Preheat the broiler on low, and spread the coconut on a cookie sheet. Broil until lightly toasted, for about 2 minutes. Meanwhile, in a mixing bowl, combine the pie filling and whipped topping just enough to marble. Spoon ¼ cup into the bottoms of four parfait glasses. Top with a heaping tablespoon of the hazelnuts, then repeat the layers. Top each evenly with any remaining filling mixture and sprinkle the tops with the toasted coconut. Serve immediately.

*STORAGE NOTE: Leftovers should be refrigerated and used
within 2 days for best quality. Do not freeze.*

Chocolate-Dipped Marshmallows

*These fun treats are great for kids to help prepare. They can
be individually wrapped to include in holiday candy tins or
to include with homemade jars of hot chocolate mix.*

Yield: 10 marshmallows

**2 cups semisweet or milk
    chocolate chips**

10 skewers or wooden dipping sticks

10 large marshmallows

Colored sugar

Place the chocolate in a medium glass bowl, and microwave on high power for 30 seconds. Stir and, if necessary to completely melt, heat for 10 seconds longer. Insert a skewer a little over halfway into each marshmallow. Hold the skewer and dip each marshmallow halfway in the chocolate. Place the colored sugar in a flat saucer and dip the marshmallow top in the sugar. Put in a glass with the skewer down, and if desired, place in the refrigerator for 3 minutes to set before serving.

*Storage Note: Leftovers should be individually wrapped in
waxed paper or candy wrapping and stored at room temperature.
Use within 2 days for best quality. Do not freeze.*

🕐 *Time-Saving Tip from Tammy*

Superfine sugar is great for dusting the tops of cookies, muffins, or even fresh sliced fruit. It is sold as ultrafine sugar (*castor sugar* is the British name) in the supermarket and has the tiniest, most uniform crystals. But there is no need to go to the extra expense of purchasing the superfine bag. Just pulse regular granulated sugar for about 30 seconds in your food processor, and you've got the same thing.

Marshmallow Fondue

It will be difficult for anyone to resist plunging into this remarkable dessert dip. I like to serve it with toasted cubes of angel food cake in addition to strawberries, bananas, or apple wedges.

Yield: 12 servings

1 (11-ounce) package butterscotch chips

4 (1-ounce) squares unsweetened chocolate, chopped

1 (14-ounce) can sweetened condensed milk

1 (7-ounce) jar marshmallow cream

¼ cup milk

1 teaspoon pure vanilla extract

Place the butterscotch chips and chocolate in a glass mixing bowl. Microwave on high power for 20 seconds. Stir and, if not completely melted and smooth, microwave for another 10 seconds. Stir in the condensed milk, marshmallow cream, and milk. Microwave in 15-second intervals until smooth. Stir in the extract, and serve warm.

STORAGE NOTE: Leftovers should be refrigerated and used within 4 days. Gently reheat in the microwave in 15-second intervals. Do not freeze.

Upside-Down Apple Pie

*Warm pie filling oozes over vanilla ice cream while covered
in a cookie "crust" and makes this dessert a keeper.*

Yield: 4 servings

1 (15-ounce) can apple pie filling

½ teaspoon pure vanilla extract

¼ teaspoon ground cinnamon

⅛ teaspoon ground nutmeg

6 shortbread cookies

1 pint vanilla ice cream

In a small saucepan over medium heat, combine the pie filling, extract, cinnamon, and nutmeg. Cook for 4 minutes, stirring occasionally.

Meanwhile, place the shortbread cookies in a heavy-duty zip-top bag and crush with a rolling pin. Scoop ice cream into individual bowls, and generously top with the warm apple mixture. Sprinkle the cookie crumbs on top, and serve immediately.

*Storage Note: Leftover pie filling can be refrigerated and used within 5 days.
Gently reheat in the microwave in 20-second intervals. Do not freeze.*

Grilled Bananas and Coconut Ice Cream

Oh, the difference a bit of grilling makes with bananas! I typically use a grill pan and do this over the stove, but feel free to utilize the outdoor grill, particularly if it is already fired up for dinner.

Yield: 4 servings

2 bananas, cut in half lengthwise
  and again crosswise

1 teaspoon rum extract, divided

1 quart coconut ice cream

½ cup caramel sauce

Place a grill pan over medium-high heat, and coat with nonstick cooking spray. Grill the bananas for 2 minutes on each side.

Place one warm banana half in the bottom of four serving bowls, and sprinkle each with ¼ teaspoon of extract. Top with a scoop of ice cream, and drizzle with the caramel sauce. Serve immediately.

NOTE: You can substitute vanilla ice cream, if desired, and sprinkle the tops with shredded coconut that has been toasted.

Apple Spiced Tea

If there ever was a need for an afternoon tea break, it's during the hectic holiday season. That just happens to coincide with my supply of apple cider in the refrigerator, but I want it warm, and this recipe is just the excuse I need to stop and take a moment to recharge.

Yield: 2 servings

1 cup water

1 cup apple cider

3 whole allspice

3 whole cloves

1 stick cinnamon

2 green tea bags

2 tablespoons light brown sugar, divided

Place the water in a glass dish, and microwave for 2 minutes on high power. Add the cider, allspice, cloves, cinnamon, and tea bags. Cover and steep for 5 minutes. Strain through a fine sieve into mugs. Discard the spices and squeeze the tea bags. Stir 1 tablespoon of the sugar into each mug, and serve warm.

Cranberry Lemonade

*This is a great nonalcoholic party drink that will appeal
to everyone who walks through your door.*

Yield: 5 cups

1 (12-ounce) can frozen
   lemonade concentrate

1 cup sparkling water or ginger ale

⅓ cup cranberry sauce

3 tablespoons orange juice

2 tablespoons lime juice

Place the lemonade concentrate, sparkling water, cranberry sauce, orange juice, and lime juice in a blender container. Fill with no more than 2 cups of ice, and process until smooth. Serve immediately.

Storage Note: Leftovers should be refrigerated and used within 4 days.

Green Onions, Eggs, and Ham

Sometimes the most basic recipes are what you crave. In this case, simple scrambled eggs take on chopped green onions, ham, and a bit of cream cheese. Tip: Do not stir the eggs constantly or you'll dry them out.

Yield: 2 servings

1 tablespoon unsalted butter

4 eggs

2 tablespoons milk

1 green onion (green part only), thinly sliced

⅓ cup chopped ham

⅛ teaspoon black pepper

2 tablespoons soft cream cheese

In a large skillet over medium heat, melt the butter. Meanwhile, whisk together the eggs, milk, onion, ham, and pepper in a bowl. Pour into the skillet, and dot evenly with small cubes of the cream cheese. Cook without stirring until the mixture sets on the bottom, for about 2 minutes. Draw a spatula across the bottom of the pan to form large curds. Continue to cook until the eggs are firm throughout, for about 2 minutes longer. Serve immediately.

NOTE: If desired, you can add 1 tablespoon of chopped fresh basil, oregano, chives, thyme, or parsley to the eggs before cooking.

🕐 *Time-Saving Tip from Tammy*

For fluffy, tender scrambled eggs, always add a tablespoon of milk for every two eggs. The fat in milk binds with the protein in eggs, giving you fabulous results. Water, on the other hand, contains no fat and tends to make the eggs tough and rubbery.

15 Minutes

Cherry Pecan Brie

I first served this appetizer for a Valentine's evening dinner. It is not just a regular for that romantic meal, but also makes appearances during the rest of the year on special occasions. If your family has never had Brie, this is a good recipe to use to make the introduction.

Yield: 8 servings

½ cup chopped pecans

1 (16-ounce) round Brie

⅓ cup cherry preserves

1 tablespoon balsamic vinegar

⅛ teaspoon salt

⅛ teaspoon black pepper

Preheat the oven to 350°F. Place the pecans on the side of an ungreased baking sheet. With a sharp knife, slice the top layer of rind off the cheese, leaving the sides and bottom intact. Place on the baking sheet beside the pecans. Cook for 5 minutes.

Meanwhile, in a small mixing bowl, stir together the preserves, vinegar, salt, and pepper. With a large spatula, transfer the softened cheese to a serving plate, and top with the cherry mixture. Top with the pecans, and serve immediately with assorted crackers.

STORAGE NOTE: Leftovers should be refrigerated and used within 4 days. Gently reheat in the microwave in 15-second intervals. Do not freeze.

Crispy Shrimp Cups

Store-bought phyllo cups that are in the freezer section are a fantastic convenience item you'll find make great appetizers. Paired with already cooked shrimp, you've got a guest-worthy snack in minutes.

Yield: 15 appetizers

1 (8-ounce) package cream cheese, softened

1 tablespoon honey

1 tablespoon minced fresh parsley

1 teaspoon hot sauce

⅛ teaspoon garlic powder

1 (1.9-ounce) package frozen phyllo cups

30 cooked salad shrimp

In a mixing bowl, combine the cream cheese, honey, parsley, hot sauce, and garlic powder until well blended. With a teaspoon, evenly distribute the cream cheese mixture into the phyllo cups and place on a serving tray. Top with 2 shrimp to form a heart shape. Serve immediately.

STORAGE NOTE: The filling will quickly make the phyllo cups soggy with prolonged storage. Place in the refrigerator for no longer than 1 day. Do not freeze.

🕐 *Time-Saving Tip from Tammy*

Don't rely on your memory when freezing foods because it will frequently fail you. Instead, make sure you label and date all food placed in the freezer. Then use the "first in, first out" rule for use based on the date.

Fried Zucchini Chips

*These fried veggies are totally addictive. Start heating the oil while
you prepare and measure the other items. If you don't have a mandolin,
slice the zucchini as thinly as you possibly can for the best results.*

Yield: 6 servings

Vegetable oil for frying
2 medium zucchini
1 egg, lightly beaten

1 cup all-purpose flour
Kosher salt

Pour 4 inches of oil in a large Dutch oven over high heat. Attach a candy thermometer, and bring the oil to 375°F.

Meanwhile, use a mandolin to slice the zucchini very thin. Place the egg and flour in separate shallow bowls. Coat the slices in egg, then dredge them in the flour. Fry the zucchini in the hot oil in batches for 2 minutes or until golden brown. Drain on paper towels, sprinkle with salt, and serve immediately.

*STORAGE NOTE: Place leftovers in an airtight container
and store at room temperature. For maximum crispness
and freshness, use within 3 days. Do not freeze.*

🕐 *Time-Saving Tip from Tammy*

Kosher salt has no additives and has an odd, irregular shape. It you looked at it under a microscope, it would resemble little triangles. This unique shape helps it dissolve quickly when it hits heat. That's why it's perfect for sprinkling on anything that has just been roasted, fried, broiled, grilled, baked, steamed, or microwaved.

Grilled Goat Cheese Asparagus

Spring is a fantastic time to grab all the fresh asparagus you can find from local farmers. Go ahead and pull out the grill for this recipe. The combination of tangy goat cheese and salty ham gives the asparagus mass appeal.

Yield: 24 appetizers

12 shaved slices country ham

4 ounces soft goat cheese

24 thin asparagus spears

Preheat the grill to medium. Meanwhile, spread each ham slice evenly with the goat cheese. Cut in half lengthwise with kitchen shears. Wrap each half with the goat cheese smear facing inward around two asparagus spears. Grill for 6 minutes (turning halfway through) or until the ham is crisp. Serve immediately.

STORAGE NOTE: Leftovers can be stored in the refrigerator for up to 2 days. Reheat under the broiler. Do not freeze.

Shoestring Parsnips

Parsnips are one of the most underutilized vegetables on the Southern landscape. Their peak in availability hits during the fall months, when you more than likely have a fryer already fired up outside. You'll love their slightly sweet flavor matched with the zippy herb salt.

Yield: 6 servings

Vegetable oil for frying
2 pounds parsnips, peeled
1 tablespoon celery salt

1 teaspoon dried dill
¼ teaspoon black pepper

Put 1 ½ inches of oil in a deep skillet, and place over medium-high heat. Attach a candy thermometer to the side of the skillet.

Meanwhile, cut the parsnips into fine julienne strips either with a knife or in a food processor fitted with the julienne disk. In a small bowl, combine the celery salt, dill, and pepper. Set aside.

When the oil reaches 375°F, add the parsnips in batches, being careful not to over-crowd the pan. Fry about 1 minute or until golden brown. Drain on paper towels and repeat with the remaining parsnips. Sprinkle with the celery salt mixture before serving.

STORAGE NOTE: Place leftovers in an airtight container and use within 2 days for best quality. Do not freeze.

Smoked Trout Stacks

This is the appetizer to make when you want things to look fancy but don't have lots of time to spend. If you can't find smoked trout, substitute smoked salmon.

Yield: 24 appetizers

1 (14-ounce) can artichoke
 hearts, drained

4 ounces cream cheese,
 softened and divided

24 hearty crackers, such as bagel chips

6 ounces smoked trout, divided
 into 24 pieces

3 tablespoons capers, drained and rinsed

Cut the artichoke hearts into thin slices. Spread the crackers with half of the cream cheese. Layer the trout and artichokes and top with a small dollop of the remaining cream cheese. Garnish with the capers and serve.

STORAGE NOTE: This recipe is not a good keeper because the crackers will become soggy. Leftovers can be unassembled and stored in the refrigerator, but should be used within 2 days.

Honey Roasted Trail Mix

Healthy snacks that are kid-friendly can coexist, and here's proof. It's perfect to pack for long car rides or for the "hungries" that hit when kids get home from school.

Yield: 8 servings

1 tablespoon unsalted butter

¼ cup honey

¼ cup slivered almonds

¼ cup coarsely chopped pecans

¼ cup coarsely chopped walnuts

¼ cup sunflower seeds

½ teaspoon ground cinnamon

¼ teaspoon salt

Dash of ground cloves

1 cup golden raisins

Place the butter in a nonstick skillet over medium-high heat. When melted, stir in the honey and cook for 2 minutes. Meanwhile, line a large jellyroll pan with aluminum foil and lightly grease with cooking spray. Set aside.

Reduce the heat to medium, and add the almonds, pecans, walnuts, sunflower seeds, cinnamon, salt, and cloves. Cook for 7 minutes, stirring frequently. Remove from the heat, and stir in the raisins. Immediately spread on the prepared jellyroll pan. Cool in the refrigerator for 2 minutes before serving warm or at room temperature.

STORAGE NOTE: Leftovers should be placed in an airtight container and stored at room temperature. Use within 1 week. Do not freeze.

Batter-Dipped Green Beans

This could be the green bean recipe your kids beg for! While beer is typically used as a popular ingredient, this one uses club soda instead, giving them a light-as-air batter.

Yield: 8 servings

4 cups peanut or canola oil

2 cups all-purpose flour

2 teaspoons paprika

1 teaspoon baking soda

½ teaspoon white pepper

¼ teaspoon onion powder

1 ¼ cups chilled club soda

½ pound trimmed green beans

Kosher salt

Place the oil in a large heavy saucepan over medium-high heat. Attach a candy thermometer to the side, and bring the oil to 375°F.

Meanwhile, in a mixing bowl, combine the flour, paprika, baking soda, white pepper, and onion powder. Make a well in the center, and gradually add the club soda, whisking until smooth. Dip the green beans one at a time in the batter and add to the hot oil. Do not overcrowd the pan, and fry in batches for 1 minute. Drain on paper towels and serve hot.

STORAGE NOTE: Leftovers should be stored in the refrigerator and used within 2 days for best quality. Reheat in a 425° oven for 4 to 5 minutes. Do not freeze.

Radish Ribbon Pickles

I discovered this recipe in a notebook of collected newspaper recipes that my mother gave me. At first, I was skeptical, but these pencil-thin slices of radishes are now my favorite way to enjoy this vegetable. Serve them as a unique appetizer with low-salt crackers and cheese, or pile them on a sandwich.

Yield: 6 servings

3 cups very thinly sliced radishes
1 teaspoon fine-grained sea salt

1 teaspoon sugar

Spread the radishes evenly on a large platter. Sprinkle with the salt and sugar. Allow to stand at room temperature for 10 minutes. Serve immediately.

STORAGE NOTE: This recipe is an excellent keeper. Place in the refrigerator and use within 1 week. Do not freeze.

Turnip Green Pesto

Okay, zip your lips on this appetizer. Let your guests taste it first and then realize how much they like this cracker spread before you spill about the ingredients. You can substitute mustard greens or collard greens for the turnip greens, if desired.

Yield: 1 cup

1 (16-ounce) bag packed fresh
   turnip greens, chopped

2 tablespoons water

2 garlic cloves

½ cup olive oil, plus more for drizzling

¼ teaspoon crushed red pepper

1 tablespoon lemon juice

¾ teaspoon salt

¼ teaspoon black pepper

1 tablespoon pine nuts

Place the turnip greens in a glass bowl and add 2 tablespoons of water. Cover with waxed paper, and microwave on high power for 4 minutes. In the meantime, mince the garlic and add to a small bowl with the ½ cup oil. Whisk in the crushed red pepper, lemon juice, salt, and pepper. Uncover the greens and drain. Transfer to the bowl of a food processor and add the oil mixture. Process until finely chopped and transfer to a chilled serving bowl. Garnish with pine nuts, and serve with assorted crackers.

*Storage Note: Leftovers should be refrigerated
and used within 4 days. Do not freeze.*

Warm Crab Dip

*The microwave comes to the rescue once more and gives you
the perfect start to a party or impromptu gathering.*

Yield: 6 cups

3 (8-ounce) packages cream cheese

1 small sweet onion, peeled and grated

½ cup mayonnaise

¼ cup chicken stock

1 tablespoon Dijon mustard

1 ½ tablespoons prepared horseradish

¾ teaspoon white pepper

½ teaspoon garlic powder

½ teaspoon seasoned salt

1 pound lump crabmeat, drained

¼ cup chopped fresh parsley

Place the cream cheese, onion, mayonnaise, stock, mustard, horseradish, white pepper, garlic powder, and seasoned salt in a glass mixing bowl. Microwave on high power for 2 minutes. Stir and heat for another 2 minutes or until the mixture has melted. Stir in the crabmeat, and transfer to a warm serving dish. Top with the parsley, and serve immediately.

*Storage Note: Leftovers should be stored in the refrigerator
and used within 3 days. Do not freeze.*

Note: This dish does well in a chafing dish to keep it warm.

Apricot and Cashew Chicken Salad

Leftover chicken sings a new song with this recipe, and you'll love the hint of sweet that the apricots bring to the dish. You can also make this salad with leftover cooked turkey, and it's just as nice.

Yield: 4 servings

2 cups diced cooked chicken

¼ cup diced celery

¼ cup mayonnaise

2 tablespoons chopped dried apricots

2 tablespoons chopped green onions

2 tablespoons chopped unsalted cashews

2 tablespoons golden raisins

2 tablespoons sour cream or plain yogurt

⅛ teaspoon salt

⅛ teaspoon black pepper

4 lettuce leaves

Chopped chives for garnish

In a large mixing bowl, combine the chicken, celery, mayonnaise, apricots, green onions, cashews, raisins, sour cream, salt, and pepper. Gently toss to mix. Place a lettuce leaf on each chilled serving plate, and top with ½ heaping cup of the chicken mixture. Sprinkle with chives and serve immediately.

STORAGE NOTE: Leftovers should be refrigerated and used within 3 days. Do not freeze.

Pecan-Topped Cream of Tomato Soup

Tomato sauce becomes tomato soup in a jiffy, and crunchy pecans garnish it perfectly. Pair this with a grilled cheese sandwich, and you've got a comfort food feast that will instantly lift your spirits. The microwave makes this meal a real quick one for when stomachs are growling!

Yield: 4 servings

12 pecan halves

2 cups chicken stock

1 cup tomato sauce

½ cup heavy cream

1 teaspoon sugar

¼ teaspoon black pepper

1 tablespoon thinly shredded fresh basil

Place the pecans on a baking sheet and put under the broiler on low. Meanwhile, combine the stock, sauce, cream, sugar, and pepper in a large glass bowl and stir to blend. Cover with waxed paper, and cook in the microwave on high power for 5 minutes.

Check the pecans, and when golden brown and fragrant, remove from the oven. Stir the soup well and ladle into individual serving bowls. Sprinkle evenly with basil leaves and pecans. Serve warm.

Storage Note: Leftovers can be refrigerated and used within 5 days. Gently reheat in the microwave for 1 minute, then in 30-second intervals. Do not freeze.

Cucumber Soup with Seafood Garnish

This is a nice soup to make and serve when the cucumber harvest is overwhelming. It is a great make-ahead recipe for summer lunches.

Yield: 4 servings

3 large cucumbers, peeled
  and roughly chopped

1 cup Greek-style yogurt

½ cup chicken or vegetable stock

⅓ cup sour cream

2 tablespoons chopped fresh chives

1 tablespoon lemon juice

1 teaspoon chopped fresh mint

½ teaspoon dry mustard

½ teaspoon salt

1 cup lump crabmeat or salad shrimp

Place the cucumbers, yogurt, stock, sour cream, chives, lemon juice, mint, dry mustard, and salt in a blender and puree until smooth. Freeze for 4 minutes. Spoon into individual serving bowls, and garnish with the crabmeat just before serving.

STORAGE NOTE: *Leftovers should be refrigerated and used within 3 days. Stir vigorously before serving. Do not freeze.*

🕐 *Time-Saving Tip from Tammy*

If you have added a bit too much salt to a soup or stew, drop in a peeled raw potato. After cooking for a few minutes, it will absorb the salty taste and can be removed and discarded before serving.

Crab and Corn Salad with Lemon Basil Dressing

This salad is fantastic and looks like it took more time to prepare than you spent on it. If you really want to fancy it up, serve scoops over thick slices of beefsteak tomatoes placed over fresh greens.

Yield: 3 servings

2 (6.5-ounce) cans lump
    crabmeat, drained

1 cup fresh whole kernel corn (2 ears)

¼ cup chopped red bell peppers

2 tablespoons thinly sliced fresh basil

2 tablespoons finely chopped red onions

¼ cup lemon juice

1 tablespoon olive oil

1 tablespoon grated lemon zest

1 teaspoon honey

½ teaspoon Dijon mustard

¼ teaspoon salt

⅛ teaspoon black pepper

In a serving bowl, combine the crab, corn, peppers, basil, and onions. Place the juice, oil, lemon zest, honey, mustard, salt, and pepper in a jar with a tight-fitting lid and shake to emulsify. Pour over the crab mixture, and toss gently to coat. Serve immediately.

Storage Note: Leftovers should be refrigerated and used within 2 days.

Note: If desired, add a cup of halved cherry tomatoes.

Tomato and Buttermilk Bisque

Start with a base of canned condensed tomato soup, and with a few simple additions, you've got a lady's lunch winner for a crowd!

Yield: 8 servings

1 (14.5-ounce) can diced
   roasted tomatoes
2 (10.75-ounce) cans condensed
   tomato soup
2 ½ cups buttermilk

2 tablespoons chopped fresh basil
2 garlic cloves, minced
¼ teaspoon black pepper
¼ cup shredded Parmesan cheese
Croutons for garnish

In a large saucepan over medium heat, stir together the tomatoes, soup, buttermilk, basil, garlic, and pepper. Cook for 7 minutes, stirring frequently. Add the Parmesan cheese, and cook for 2 minutes longer. Ladle into warm soup bowls, and garnish with croutons. Serve immediately.

STORAGE NOTE: Leftovers should be refrigerated and used within 4 days. Gently reheat in the microwave for 1 minute, then at 30-second intervals. Do not freeze.

Fennel Salad with Onions and Oranges

From fall through spring, local fennel is available, and this salad showcases this often neglected beauty. Don't overlook the fragrant, graceful fronds at the top, which can be snipped like dill and used as a last-minute flavor enhancer. This is a great side salad for fish or simple baked chicken.

Yield: 6 servings

3 fennel bulbs, cored, trimmed, and very thinly sliced

½ purple onion, peeled and very thinly sliced

1 orange, peeled and cut in pieces

2 tablespoons olive oil

2 tablespoons lemon juice

1 tablespoon chopped fennel fronds

¼ teaspoon salt

⅛ teaspoon black pepper

In a large serving bowl, toss together the fennel, onions, and oranges. In a jar with a tight-fitting lid, combine the oil, juice, fennel fronds, salt, and pepper. Shake to emulsify, and pour over the fennel mixture. Serve at room temperature.

STORAGE NOTE: Leftovers should be refrigerated and used within 3 days. Do not freeze.

Just Peachy Turkey Salad

Fresh peaches that are peeled and sliced very thin make a great addition to any green salad. Here, I like the bonus of using leftover cooked turkey. If you want, substitute prosciutto or roasted chicken.

Yield: 4 servings

1 (6-ounce) package spring green salad mix

1 (8-ounce) package fresh mozzarella, sliced

2 large fresh peaches, peeled and thinly sliced

2 cups chopped cooked turkey

½ cup olive oil

¼ cup lemon juice

½ tablespoon chopped fresh thyme

¼ teaspoon salt

⅛ teaspoon black pepper

Distribute the greens evenly on 4 chilled salad plates. Evenly top with the mozzarella, peaches, and turkey. In a jar with a tight-fitting lid, combine the oil, lemon juice, thyme, salt, and pepper. Shake to emulsify. Drizzle over each salad and serve immediately.

STORAGE NOTE: Leftovers should be refrigerated and used within 3 days.

Farmer's Market Shrimp Gazpacho

This summer soup is inexpensive, yet filling and delicious when you utilize a garden harvest for the fresh ingredients. It keeps well in the refrigerator, making it a great do-ahead meal, or it can be served instantly for a quick lunch. Just add crusty bread and you're ready to eat.

Yield: 6 servings

1 large cucumber, halved lengthwise and cut into large chunks

1 red bell pepper, halved and seeded

1 medium onion, peeled and halved

2 large tomatoes, cored and halved

3 cups tomato juice, divided

3 garlic cloves

⅓ cup red wine vinegar

⅓ cup olive oil

½ teaspoon salt

¼ teaspoon black pepper

½ teaspoon hot sauce

12 cooked medium shrimp

In a food processor, combine half the cucumbers, half the bell pepper, half the onion, one of the tomatoes, and one cup of the tomato juice. Puree until smooth, and pour into a large serving bowl. Set aside.

Process the remaining cucumbers, bell pepper, onion, tomato, and garlic until finely chopped. Add to the serving bowl and stir in the remaining juice, vinegar, oil, salt, pepper, and hot sauce. Freeze for 2 minutes. Arrange two shrimp in the shape of a heart on the bottom of each bowl and allow guests to serve themselves with a generous topping of gazpacho.

STORAGE NOTE: Leftovers should be refrigerated and used within 3 days or frozen and used within 1 month.

Mushroom and Vidalia Onion Soup

I love making this soup in the fall and serving it outside around the fire with loaves of crusty bread. Purchase already sliced mushrooms to speed along the preparation.

Yield: 2 servings

2 tablespoons unsalted butter

1 sweet onion, peeled and sliced

¾ pound sliced mushrooms

¼ cup water

1 (14.5-ounce) can chicken stock

½ teaspoon garlic salt

¼ teaspoon black pepper

1 tablespoon chopped fresh chives

Place the butter in a large saucepan over medium-high heat. When melted and foamy, add the onions and mushrooms, and sauté for 4 minutes, stirring frequently. Add the water, stock, salt, and pepper, and bring to a boil, stirring frequently. Boil for 4 minutes, and remove from the heat. Ladle into warm soup bowls, and serve with a garnish of fresh chives.

STORAGE NOTE: Leftovers should be refrigerated and used within 5 days or frozen and used within 1 month.

NOTE: Add a cup of cooked chopped chicken, ham, or turkey to the soup when you add the stock, if desired.

◷ Time-Saving Tip from Tammy

Want to stuff a tomato and summer squash? Use a melon baller! A small one is also great for pulling out the gills and inside stems of fresh mushrooms.

Nip and Sip Peanut Soup

It took me awhile to warm up to the idea of peanut soup. But the instant I tried it for the first time, I was hooked. This one is perfect for sipping at lunch!

Yield: 6 servings

3 cups milk

1 teaspoon finely chopped onion

½ teaspoon salt

¼ teaspoon white pepper

1 tablespoon flour

¼ cup chicken stock

½ cup smooth peanut butter

¼ cup crushed unsalted or lightly salted peanuts for garnish

Paprika for garnish

Place the milk, onion, salt, and pepper in a heavy saucepan over medium-high heat. Bring to a simmer while you measure the remaining ingredients. In a mixing bowl, combine the flour and stock, stirring until smooth. Stir in the peanut butter until thoroughly combined. Add to the milk mixture and heat for 7 minutes, stirring constantly. Serve warm with a garnish of peanuts and a sprinkling of paprika.

Storage Note: Leftovers should be refrigerated and used within 4 days. Gently reheat in the microwave for 1 minute, then at 30-second intervals. Do not freeze.

Tomato, Onion, and Cucumber Salad

I like to use sweet onions in this recipe, but stronger regular onions will work if that's what you have on hand. You might want to cut the amount used in half to compensate for the more prominent flavor.

Yield: 6 servings

3 tomatoes, sliced

1 sweet onion, peeled and thinly sliced

1 large cucumber, peeled
   and thinly sliced

½ cup halved cherry tomatoes

¼ cup white wine vinegar

¼ cup olive oil

½ teaspoon salt

½ teaspoon black pepper

1 tablespoon fresh chopped chives

Arrange the tomato slices on a serving platter and set aside. In a medium bowl, combine the onion, cucumber, and cherry tomatoes. In a jar with a tight-fitting lid, combine the vinegar, oil, salt, and pepper. Shake to emulsify, and pour over the onion mixture. Spoon over the sliced tomatoes, and garnish with the chives.

STORAGE NOTE: Leftovers should be refrigerated and used within 4 days. Do not freeze.

Carrot "Fries"

Who says potatoes have to rule the world of "fries"? Everyday carrots can be turned into a great side dish for sandwiches and can go into the oven even before it finishes preheating. Use kosher salt in this recipe so that it will practically melt into the carrots as they cook.

Yield: 4 servings

1 pound carrot sticks, cut in half lengthwise

2 teaspoons olive oil

½ teaspoon kosher salt

⅛ teaspoon white pepper

Preheat the oven to 450°F. Lightly coat a jellyroll pan with cooking spray, and arrange the carrots in a single layer. Drizzle with the oil and sprinkle evenly with the salt and pepper. Place in the middle of the oven even if it hasn't completed preheating. Bake for 10 minutes or until golden brown, and serve hot.

STORAGE NOTE: Leftovers should be refrigerated and used within 2 days. Reheat under the broiler. Do not freeze.

🕐 *Time-Saving Tip from Tammy*

Roasting vegetables in the oven while you bake a casserole or meat makes the oven a multitasking appliance. For the best results, cut the vegetables in uniform sizes for even cooking. Then to make sure they brown on both sides, turn them with a spatula halfway through the roasting time. Do not stack the vegetables, but place them in a single layer, and use a pan that has shallow sides. A jelly roll pan works best.

Hand-Mashed Turnips

Before you turn your nose up at this recipe, give it a try. The combination of turnips and potatoes sings, and it's a real cost-saver to boot.

Yield: 6 servings

2 pounds turnips, peeled and cut into 1-inch pieces

½ pound Yukon gold potatoes, peeled and cut into 1-inch pieces

3 tablespoons unsalted butter

3 tablespoons heavy cream

½ teaspoon salt

¼ teaspoon black pepper

Put the turnips and potatoes in a large saucepan and cover with water. Place over high heat and boil for 7 minutes. Drain well, and add the butter, cream, salt, and pepper. Coarsely mash with a potato masher, and adjust the seasonings if necessary. Serve warm.

Storage Note: Leftovers should be refrigerated and used within 4 days. A tablespoon of milk or cream should be added upon reheating. Warm in the microwave for 1 minute, then at 15-second intervals. Leftovers can be frozen, but separation may occur, so when thawed and reheating as instructed above, whisk well to blend. Use frozen leftovers within 1 month for best quality.

Herbed Squash

This recipe helps use up those mountains of zucchini and yellow squash that seem to overwhelm gardeners around mid-summer. I love this with lamb chops or barbecue.

Yield: 4 servings

1 tablespoon olive oil
1 cup julienned zucchini
1 cup julienned yellow squash
½ cup shelled edamame
1 teaspoon minced fresh basil
1 teaspoon minced fresh thyme

1 teaspoon minced fresh sage or rosemary
½ teaspoon crushed red pepper
½ teaspoon white pepper
4 tablespoons crumbled Feta cheese

Place the oil in a heavy skillet over medium-high heat. Add the zucchini, squash, edamame, basil, thyme, sage, red pepper, and white pepper. Cook for 5 minutes, stirring frequently. Sprinkle with the Feta cheese, and serve immediately.

STORAGE NOTE: Leftovers should be refrigerated and used within 4 days. Do not freeze.

🕐 *Time-Saving Tip from Tammy*

Fresh herbs are not always readily available in a busy kitchen. Dried can be substituted, but decrease the amount by one-third. So if a recipe calls for 1 tablespoon of fresh herbs, you can use 1 teaspoon of dried instead.

Hoppin' John

This is my comfort food of choice, and it's nice to know that you don't have to slave over a hot stove to make this soothing recipe. This one still has traditional flavor, but comes together quickly.

Yield: 3 cups

2 tablespoons bacon drippings
  or vegetable oil

1 cup diced sweet onions

1 (8.8-ounce) package
  ready-to-serve rice

1 (15-ounce) can black-
  eyed peas, drained

¼ teaspoon garlic powder

¼ teaspoon black pepper

¼ teaspoon cayenne

Place the drippings in a large skillet over medium-high heat. Add the onions, and sauté for 5 minutes or until golden. Meanwhile, cook the rice in the microwave according to the package directions. Stir in the cooked rice, black-eyed peas, garlic powder, black pepper, and cayenne. Cook for 5 minutes longer or until heated through. Serve warm.

STORAGE NOTE: Leftovers should be refrigerated and used within 4 days. Do not freeze.

Red Pepper Corn

This recipe takes me back in time. I remember when the combination of corn and red peppers hit the market in the canned form. This one uses fresh ingredients and is lovely.

Yield: 4 servings

3 cups fresh whole kernel corn

⅓ cup finely chopped red bell peppers

2 tablespoons water

2 tablespoons honey

¾ teaspoon salt

½ teaspoon chili powder

¼ teaspoon white pepper

Place the corn, peppers, and water in a glass bowl and cover with waxed paper. Microwave on high power for 9 minutes. Drain, and stir in the honey, salt, chili powder, and pepper. Serve hot.

STORAGE NOTE: This recipe freezes beautifully. Use within 3 months for best quality. Refrigerated leftovers should be used within 4 days.

⏲ *Time-Saving Tip from Tammy*

Honey or sorghum syrup will eventually crystallize if left on the pantry shelf too long, but don't throw it away. Instead, place the opened jar in the microwave and heat on high power for 10 seconds. Stir until melted, and it's ready to use again. If it has formed a lot of crystals, you may need to heat it for another 10 seconds.

Sauced Carrots

The next time you serve grilled fish, pull out this recipe. It is one of my favorite food pairings. A bonus is that both are quick to the table!

Yield: 6 servings

½ cup (1 stick) unsalted butter
½ teaspoon salt

12 carrots, peeled and sliced
½ cup beef stock

Place the butter in a heavy saucepan over medium-high heat. When bubbly, add the salt and carrots. Cook for 2 minutes. Add the stock, cover, and reduce the heat to medium. Continue cooking for 8 minutes or until the carrots are tender. Serve warm.

STORAGE NOTE: Leftovers should be refrigerated and used within 4 days. For longer storage, freeze and use within 3 months.

Seasoned Green Beans

*Canned beans are a must on pantry shelves. They are instant side
dishes in themselves, but this one gets some help from ordinary
staples and can be served cold, warm, or at room temperature.*

Yield: 4 servings

1 (16-ounce) can green beans, drained

1 tablespoon rice vinegar

1 tablespoon water or vegetable stock

1 heaping tablespoon minced shallots

¼ teaspoon black pepper

2 teaspoons bacon bits

Place the green beans in a serving bowl. Toss gently with the vinegar, water, shallots, and pepper. Let stand at room temperature for 10 minutes. Sprinkle with the bacon bits and serve, or place in the microwave and cook on high power for 2 minutes and serve warm.

*Storage Note: Leftovers should be refrigerated and used within
4 days. Or you can freeze them and use within 1 month.*

Spice Cabinet Okra

This recipe takes ordinary okra to an elegant level and utilizes some spices that you might not regularly reach for in your spice cabinet. Serving this spicy side with the cold garnish is a wake-up call for your mouth.

Yield: 5 servings

1 teaspoon mustard seeds

1 teaspoon turmeric

½ teaspoon ground coriander

½ teaspoon ground cumin

¼ teaspoon red pepper flakes

¼ teaspoon black pepper

1 small sweet onion, peeled and diced

3 cups fresh okra, cut in thirds on the bias

½ cup plain nonfat Greek yogurt or sour cream

Coat a wok with cooking spray and place over medium-high heat. Add the mustard seeds, turmeric, coriander, cumin, red pepper flakes, and black pepper. Cook, stirring constantly, for 2 minutes or until the seeds pop. Carefully add the onions, and cook for 2 minutes longer, stirring constantly.

Increase the heat to high, and add the okra. Cook, stirring occasionally, for 2 minutes more. Serve immediately with a tablespoon of the cold yogurt on the side.

Storage Note: Leftovers should be refrigerated and used within 3 days. Do not freeze.

Smashed Potatoes

Mashed potatoes are actually nothing more than a puree that is enhanced with butter, milk, salt, and pepper. Once again, the microwave comes to our quick rescue by making these go from an hour to prepare to merely minutes. Increase the amount of milk if you like softer, creamier potatoes.

Yield: 4 servings

2 large baking potatoes (8 ounces each)

⅓ cup milk

2 tablespoons unsalted butter

½ teaspoon salt

¼ teaspoon black pepper

Prick the potatoes generously with a fork and place on a plate. Microwave on high power for 11 minutes. Meanwhile, place the milk, butter, salt, and pepper in a glass bowl. Remove the potatoes with a pot holder and cut into large chunks. Push through a ricer or mash with a potato masher in the butter bowl. Stir until the butter melts. Adjust seasonings if necessary, and serve warm.

STORAGE NOTE: Leftovers should be refrigerated and used within 4 days. Freezing for up to 1 month is acceptable, but separation will occur. Upon thawing and reheating, whisk the potatoes well and add a tablespoon of milk or cream to enhance the consistency.

Sugar-Glazed Pearl Onions

*It wasn't until later in life that I gained an appreciation for pearl onions.
Until then, they were items to be picked out of English peas. Now I like to
serve them as an unusual side dish with anything from fish to wild game.
Leftovers can be added to hot buttered noodles for dinner on the run.*

Yield: 6 servings

1 (16-ounce) package frozen pearl onions

2 tablespoons unsalted butter

3 tablespoons light brown sugar

1 tablespoon Dijon mustard

⅛ teaspoon white pepper

2 tablespoons chopped fresh parsley

Bring a large pot of water to a boil over high heat. Add the onions and cook for 2 minutes. Drain, and plunge into ice water. Pinch the root end, and the outer peel will slip off. Place the butter in a large skillet over medium-high heat, and add the onions as they are peeled. Cook for 2 minutes and add the brown sugar, mustard, and pepper. Cook for 2 minutes longer. Sprinkle with parsley, and serve hot.

*STORAGE NOTE: Leftovers should be refrigerated
and used within 5 days. Do not freeze.*

Maple Butter Squash

*Spotlight this side dish during the fall and winter months when all
hard-shelled squash varieties, including acorn squash, are abundant
and inexpensive. Serve with grilled fish or roasted pork.*

Yield: 2 servings

1 acorn squash, halved and seeded

1 tablespoon water

1 tablespoon unsalted butter

¼ cup maple syrup

2 tablespoons chopped pecans

Place the squash in a glass baking dish with the cut side up, and add 1 tablespoon of water into the dish. Cover with waxed paper, and microwave on high power for 10 minutes. Remove, and place ½ tablespoon of butter in the center of each squash half. Spoon 2 tablespoons of syrup over the butter, and sprinkle each with a tablespoon of the pecans. Serve warm.

*STORAGE NOTE: Leftovers should be refrigerated
and used within 4 days. Do not freeze.*

Just Right Mushrooms

*The first time I had these, they were served with Melba toast as an appetizer.
I fell in love with them, but have transformed the recipe into a terrific
side dish. Any leftovers can be thrown onto hot cooked pasta or rice.*

Yield: 4 servings

2 yellow onions, peeled and quartered

¾ cup water

½ cup distilled white vinegar

½ cup beef consommé or stock

2 tablespoons unsalted butter

1 teaspoon salt

½ teaspoon celery seeds

½ teaspoon mustard seeds

1 pound whole fresh mushrooms

¼ cup olive oil

In a large saucepan over high heat, combine the onions, water, vinegar, consommé, butter, salt, celery seeds, and mustard seeds. Bring to a boil and cook for 3 minutes. Add the mushrooms and simmer for 5 minutes. Remove the mushrooms with tongs and place in a serving bowl. Strain the liquid, discarding the solids. Add the oil to the strained liquid, and pour over the mushrooms. Toss gently and serve warm.

*STORAGE NOTE: Leftovers should be refrigerated and used within
4 days. Or you can freeze and use within 1 month.*

🕐 *Time-Saving Tip from Tammy*

Most of us use kitchen tongs for flipping meat, but they have other uses, as well. Use tongs with silicone tips to remove ramekins from their water bath. They are also terrific for removing hot lids from bubbling pots.

Balsamic and Garlic Sautéed Kale

*This nutrient-rich leafy green is a great side dish. The stems
of kale should always be discarded because they are tough.
Use the best balsamic vinegar you can afford.*

Yield: 4 servings

3 tablespoons peanut oil

4 garlic cloves, minced

1 large yellow onion, peeled
   and coarsely chopped

1 ½ pounds kale

½ cup chicken stock

1 tablespoon balsamic vinegar

½ teaspoon salt

Place the oil in a large sauté pan over medium heat. Add the garlic and onions, and
sauté for 3 minutes. Add half of the kale leaves and when wilted, add the remaining
leaves. Add the stock; cover and cook for 8 minutes or until the liquid has evaporated.
Stir in the balsamic vinegar and salt, and serve warm.

*STORAGE NOTE: Leftovers should be refrigerated
and used within 2 days. Do not freeze.*

Butter-Fried Corn

Fresh corn needs very little to enhance the sweet flavor. Cut the kernels from the cobs as you melt the butter. It is exquisite with any main dish.

Yield: 6 servings

2 tablespoons unsalted butter
6 ears fresh corn, husked and silked

1 tablespoon heavy cream

Place the butter in a large skillet over medium heat. Cut the kernels from the cobs and add to the skillet, along with the cream. Cook, stirring occasionally, for 10 minutes. Serve warm.

Storage Note: Leftovers should be refrigerated and used within 3 days or frozen and used within 1 month.

🕐 *Time-Saving Tip from Tammy*

Look at corn husks as nature's freshness seal. They help keep valuable moisture next to the kernels, as well as keeping them cool. Don't remove them until just before you are ready to prepare the corn.

Peanut Vegetable Stir-Fry

Barely cooked vegetables are fantastic for getting sides on the table fast. A wok is just as valuable as the microwave for quick cooking. For fun, use colored carrots in white, red, yellow, or purple. Also, vary the mushroom varieties and substitute cauliflower for broccoli if you want.

Yield: 6 servings

2 tablespoons peanut oil

2 medium carrots, thinly sliced

2 cups broccoli florets

2 cups sliced fresh mushrooms

1 cup shelled edamame

1 tablespoon white wine vinegar

½ teaspoon onion or garlic salt

¼ teaspoon dried oregano

¼ teaspoon black pepper

1 tablespoon fresh snipped chives

¼ cup unsalted peanuts

Heat the oil over high heat in a large bowl-shaped skillet or wok. Add the carrots and broccoli, and cook for 2 minutes, stirring constantly. Add the mushrooms and edamame. Cook for 2 minutes longer, stirring frequently. Stir in the vinegar, and sprinkle with the salt, oregano, and pepper. Cook for 1 minute longer. Transfer to a serving dish, and top with the chives and peanuts. Serve immediately.

STORAGE NOTE: Leftovers should be refrigerated and used within 4 days. Do not freeze.

NOTE: Turn this side dish into a meal by serving it over hot cooked rice.

Sautéed Spinach

This spinach side dish provides you a much needed break from everyday vegetables. It's elegant, easy, and nutrient-packed. Serve it with seafood or roasted pork. If desired, top the spinach with a bit of mozzarella cheese before serving.

Yield: 6 servings

2 tablespoons olive oil

3 garlic cloves, minced

¼ cup beef consommé or stock

1 (18-ounce) package fresh
baby spinach leaves

¾ teaspoon salt

¼ teaspoon cayenne

Place the oil in a large skillet over medium-high heat. Add the garlic, and sauté for 30 seconds. Add the consommé, and bring to a boil. Add the spinach, salt, and cayenne. Cover and cook for 4 to 5 minutes or until wilted. Serve hot with a slotted spoon.

STORAGE NOTE: Leftovers should be refrigerated and used within 4 days. Do not freeze.

Buttered Spinach Noodles

This dish became a favorite of mine when I got together with my friend Sally. We didn't have a lot of money, and this fit our tight budgets to a tee. It is still a go-to dish when I am craving something deliciously simple. You can add any leftover cooked, chopped meat or vegetables if you want to fancy it up, but I think it's perfect just as it is.

Yield: 2 servings

2 ½ cups egg noodles

1 cup baby spinach

2 tablespoons unsalted butter, softened

2 teaspoons chopped fresh parsley

¼ teaspoon garlic salt

¼ teaspoon black pepper

Cook the noodles in boiling water according to the package directions. Meanwhile, place the spinach, butter, parsley, salt, and pepper in a serving bowl. Drain the pasta and transfer to the serving bowl. Toss to coat, and serve warm.

STORAGE NOTE: Leftovers should be refrigerated and used within 5 days. Do not freeze.

Cornmeal Crusted Chicken

Plain cornmeal becomes a crispy coating for boneless chicken breasts. Serve this with Raw Tomato Compote (page 93) on the side and a green salad.

Yield: 2 servings

2 tablespoons unsalted butter

1 tablespoon canola or vegetable oil

1 large, whole, boneless, skinless chicken breast, cut in half horizontally

¼ cup yellow cornmeal

¼ teaspoon paprika

¼ teaspoon cayenne

¼ teaspoon black pepper

Place the butter and oil in a large skillet over medium-high heat. Meanwhile, put the chicken breasts in a large zip-top bag and add the cornmeal, paprika, cayenne, and black pepper. Seal the bag and shake to evenly coat. Add the crusted chicken halves to the hot skillet. Cook for about 5 minutes on each side or until cooked through and golden brown. Serve warm.

STORAGE NOTE: Leftovers can be frozen and used within 2 months. Thaw in the refrigerator, and reheat in a 450° oven for 12 to 15 minutes, turning halfway through. Or you can refrigerate leftovers and use within 3 days. Use the same reheating instructions above.

🕐 *Time-Saving Tip from Tammy*

Boneless, skinless chicken breasts are good time savers, but cost more than split breasts that have the skin still attached. The skin has a useful purpose and helps keep the meat from drying out during cooking or grilling. So don't avoid it at the meat case. Just remove the skin after the recipe is complete and the meat will be juicy and moist.

Great Grilling

I like to grill year-round, and so do many others. I can get dinner on the table in a hurry with little effort or kitchen mess to deal with afterward. While you may prefer a terrific marinade on the weekends, rushed weeknights rarely provide time for that option. So just sprinkle the meat liberally with salt and pepper, and you've got dinner.

Yield: 4 servings

1 teaspoon salt   **½ teaspoon black pepper**

Meat options below

Preheat the grill to medium-high. Meanwhile, sprinkle the salt and pepper on both sides of the meat option selected. Grill according to the guidelines suggested, and serve warm.

MEAT OPTIONS:		
Rib-Eye Steaks	4 1-inch thick	Grill for 4 to 5 minutes on each side for medium-rare.
Pork Chops	4 center cut with bone in and no more than ¾-inch thick	Grill for 6 to 7 minutes on each side or until a thermometer registers 160°F.
Lamb Chops	4 1-inch thick	Grill for 4 minutes on each side for medium-rare.
Chicken Breast	4 boneless, skinless and no more than ½ pound each	Grill for 4 minutes on each side or until a thermometer registers 160°F.
Chicken Thighs	4 boneless and skinless	Grill for 4 minutes on each side or until a thermometer registers 160°F.
Fish Steaks (such as halibut)	4 1-inch thick and no more than ½ pound each	Grill for 3 ½ minutes on each side or until the flesh is opaque.
Tuna Steaks	4 1-inch thick and no more than ½ pound each	Grill for 2 ½ minutes on each side for medium.

STORAGE NOTE: All of these leftover grilled options can be refrigerated or frozen. Use refrigerated leftover fish within 2 days, and the remaining options within 4 days. For the best quality, use frozen leftover fish within 1 month, and the remaining options within 2 months.

⏱ *Time-Saving Tip from Tammy*

Take the meat out of the refrigerator 10 minutes before you're ready to cook. This takes the chill off and allows the meat to cook in the time called for in the recipe.

Sesame Dilled Catfish

*Being from Mississippi, I love catfish and have found dozens of
ways to cook this farm-raised, quick-cooking fish. This one gets a
touch of easy elegance with the addition of sesame seeds.*

Yield: 4 servings

¼ cup vegetable oil

½ cup dry seasoned breadcrumbs

¼ cup sesame seeds

½ teaspoon dried dill

¼ teaspoon salt

¼ teaspoon white pepper

¾ cup plain yogurt or sour cream

1 pound (4- to 5-ounce) catfish fillets

Lemon wedges

Pour the oil in a large skillet over medium-high heat. Meanwhile, put the bread-crumbs, sesame seeds, dill, salt, and pepper in a shallow dish. Place the yogurt in a separate shallow dish. Dredge the fillets in the yogurt, then in the breadcrumb mixture. Fry in the hot oil for 3 minutes on each side or until the fish flakes easily with a fork. Serve warm with lemon wedges.

STORAGE NOTE: *These leftovers should not be frozen, but can
be refrigerated and used within a couple of days.*

🕐 *Time-Saving Tip from Tammy*

Rule of thumb: Fish requires no more than 10 minutes total cooking time for each inch of thickness. That includes any breading or batters you add to the fish.

Zippy Chicken and "Gravy"

I never hesitate to utilize the supermarket butcher for slicing, and this recipe can take full advantage of that relationship. By slicing the chicken breasts in half, you drastically reduce the cooking time, and the mock gravy is created with pan drippings.

Yield: 4 servings

2 tablespoons unsalted butter

¼ cup all-purpose flour

¼ teaspoon white pepper

1 pound boneless, skinless chicken breasts, sliced in half lengthwise

¼ cup white wine Worcestershire sauce

2 tablespoons half-and-half or milk

Place the butter in a large skillet over medium heat to melt. Meanwhile, put the flour and pepper in a large zip-top bag. Add the chicken, half at a time, and shake to dredge. Add to the skillet and lightly brown for 3 minutes on each side. Shift the chicken around halfway through the cooking so it doesn't stick to the skillet.

Remove to a serving bowl and cover with aluminum foil to keep warm. Add the Worcestershire sauce and half-and half to the skillet. With a wooden spoon, scrape the bottom of the skillet. Cook for 2 minutes. Pour over the chicken, and serve immediately.

STORAGE NOTE: *Leftovers should be refrigerated and used within 3 days.*

Seven-Layer Chicken and Vegetables

I used to make a traditional seven-layer salad all the time, but began to cut back on that heavy layer of mayonnaise several years ago. In this updated version of the Southern classic, I eliminate it totally and don't miss it a bit, thanks to the zesty dressing. Use a large, somewhat shallow bowl for this presentation.

Yield: 6 servings

5 cups shredded lettuce

1 (3-ounce) package plain
  ramen noodles

1 orange bell pepper, seeded and diced

2 cups diced cooked chicken or turkey

1 (11-ounce) can yellow and
  white corn, drained

3 Roma tomatoes, diced

3 green onions, sliced

¼ cup canola or vegetable oil

3 tablespoons red wine vinegar

1 tablespoon sugar

1 teaspoon garlic salt

½ teaspoon black pepper

Arrange the lettuce on the bottom of a 3-quart glass serving dish. Coarsely break the noodles and scatter over the lettuce. Layer the bell pepper, chicken, corn, tomatoes, and onions over the top.

In a jar with a tight-fitting lid, combine the oil, vinegar, sugar, salt, and pepper. Shake to emulsify, and pour over the salad. Serve immediately, or cover and refrigerate for use within an hour.

Storage Note: These leftovers should not be frozen, but can be refrigerated and used within a couple of days.

Carolina Creamed Chicken

I'm fairly certain this recipe was created just for the excuse of making biscuits at a time other than breakfast. I have a friend who likes it over rice and another who prefers it over thick, toasted bread. Regardless of how you serve it, this dish is just about as Southern as a recipe can get.

Yield: 8 servings

3 tablespoons unsalted butter

8 ounces fresh sliced mushrooms

¼ cup finely chopped red or
   orange bell peppers

¼ cup chopped green onions

¼ cup all-purpose flour

1 teaspoon garlic salt

⅛ teaspoon black pepper

1 ¾ cups half-and-half

2 cups chicken stock

3 cups cooked chopped chicken

Place the butter in a large saucepan over medium-high heat. Add the mushrooms, peppers, and onions, and cook for 5 minutes. Stir in the flour, salt, and pepper. Reduce the heat to medium-low, and gradually stir in the half-and-half and stock. Stir constantly until the mixture is thick, for around 1 minute. Add the chicken, and cook for 1 minute longer. Serve warm over split biscuits, toast, or hot cooked rice.

STORAGE NOTE: Tightly cover any leftovers and refrigerate.
Use within 3 days for the best quality. Do not freeze.

Spice-Rubbed Fried Pork Chops

The key to having this entrée ready in minutes is to have the oil hot, but not smoking. This rub mixture can easily be adapted with similar spices in your pantry.

Yield: 2 servings

2 tablespoons canola or vegetable oil

1 teaspoon dried chives

1 teaspoon dried thyme leaves

1 large garlic clove, minced

½ teaspoon paprika

¼ teaspoon black pepper

2 (¾-inch thick) pork chops

Place the oil in a large, heavy skillet over medium heat. Meanwhile, in a small bowl, combine the chives, thyme, garlic, paprika, and black pepper. Rub on both sides of the pork chops. Add the pork to the hot skillet, and cook for 5 minutes on each side. Serve warm.

STORAGE NOTE: These pork chops freeze beautifully. Use within 2 months for the best quality. For easy servings, individually wrap the leftovers in aluminum foil and place in a freezer-quality zip-top bag. Then you can pull the appropriate number from the freezer as needed. Refrigerated leftovers should be used within 4 days.

Spiced Potato-Crusted Catfish

A box of mashed potato flakes was the inspiration for this catfish delight. It mimics deep-fried fish, thanks to the crispy texture, but is quickly panfried instead.

Yield: 6 servings

¼ cup vegetable oil

2 eggs, beaten

1 ½ cups mashed potato flakes

1 teaspoon dried thyme

½ teaspoon garlic powder

½ teaspoon onion salt

¼ teaspoon black pepper

⅛ teaspoon paprika

6 (5-ounce) catfish fillets

Lemon wedges

Heat the oil in a large skillet over medium-high heat. Meanwhile, place the eggs in a shallow dish. Combine the potato flakes, thyme, garlic powder, salt, pepper, and paprika in a separate shallow dish. Dredge the fillets in the eggs, then in the potato mixture. Panfry in the hot oil for 4 minutes on each side. Serve warm with lemon wedges.

STORAGE NOTE: Refrigerated leftovers should be used within 2 days. Reheat and crisp up by placing the fillets under a low broiler, turning for even browning. Do not freeze.

Stuffed Hamburgers

*The first time I had these vegetable-packed burgers at a restaurant, I was hooked.
I have recreated that meal, and it's now one of our routine weeknight dinners.*

Yield: 4 servings

1 ¼ pounds ground beef

½ cup chopped roasted red bell peppers

½ cup shredded mozzarella cheese

½ teaspoon onion or garlic salt

¼ teaspoon black pepper

4 hamburger buns

2 tablespoons spicy or plain mayonnaise

4 lettuce leaves

Preheat the broiler to high. Lightly grease a wire rack and place over a jellyroll pan. Set aside.

Divide the beef into 8 equal portions and flatten into patties. Sprinkle 4 of the patties with 2 tablespoons each of the peppers and cheese. Sprinkle evenly with the salt and pepper. Top with the remaining patties, and work around the edges to seal completely with the meat. Place on the prepared pan, and broil for 5 minutes per side.

While the burgers cook, spread the hamburger buns with mayonnaise and place a lettuce leaf on each top bun. When cooked, place the burger on the bottom half and cover with the top half. Serve immediately.

STORAGE NOTE: *These leftovers freeze beautifully. Use within 2 months for the best quality. Or you can refrigerate the leftovers and use within 4 days.*

NOTE: *To test for doneness, do not insert an instant-read thermometer into the center since the burger is stuffed. Instead, make a small cut into the meat to make sure no pink remains.*

⏱ *Time-Saving Tip from Tammy*

Tired of the same old hamburger buns? Then select ciabatta rolls from the supermarket deli the next time you want to elevate the meal. While you are there, select some cheeses you don't normally purchase. Just a few slices from the deli counter will allow you to see if you like the variety without having to invest in a large quantity.

Turkey and Cranberry Sandwiches

It just wouldn't be the day after Thanksgiving without leftover turkey slices to be turned into yummy sandwiches. And perhaps this recipe will make you decide to roast that bird on a more regular basis!

Yield: 3 sandwiches

6 sourdough bread slices

2 ½ ounces spreadable blue cheese

¾ pound sliced turkey

¼ cup whole-berry cranberry sauce

1 cup loosely packed arugula

2 tablespoons mayonnaise

Preheat the broiler to high. Place the bread slices on an ungreased baking sheet, and toast for 2 minutes or until light golden brown. Remove from the oven and cool on the baking sheet for 1 minute. Reduce the broiler to low.

Spread 3 slices of the bread with the blue cheese. Top evenly with the turkey, cranberry sauce, and arugula. Spread the other half of the bread slices with mayonnaise and top the sandwiches. Place on the baking sheet and return to the oven for 1 minute on each side. Cut in half on the diagonal, and serve immediately.

Warm Apple Pie Sauce

A stainless steel apple wedger not only slices an apple but cores it at the same time. It is an easy and quick way to prepare apples for this recipe or just to enjoy as a fast snack.

Yield: 6 servings

4 tablespoons unsalted butter

½ cup packed dark brown sugar

4 Gala or Granny Smith apples, cored and cut into 8 wedges each

¼ cup golden raisins

½ cup apple cider

½ teaspoon ground cinnamon

Place the butter in a large skillet over high heat. Stir in the sugar and cook for 1 minute. Add the apples, and sprinkle with the raisins. Cook undisturbed for 6 minutes. Add the cider and cinnamon, and bring to a boil. Cook for 1 minute. Serve warm.

STORAGE NOTE: Leftovers should be refrigerated and used within 4 days. Gently reheat in the microwave for 1 minute, then at 15-second intervals. Do not freeze.

Toffee Chip Chocolate Cream Pie

This creamy pie has a toffee chip crunch and is a heavenly way to end any meal. Toffee chips are found in the baking aisle alongside chocolate chips.

Yield: 8 servings

1 (8-ounce) package cream cheese

½ cup sugar

⅓ cup cocoa powder

⅓ cup milk or heavy cream

1 teaspoon pure vanilla extract

Chocolate cookie crust

½ cup toffee chips, divided

1 (8-ounce) container frozen whipped topping, thawed

Place the cream cheese in a glass mixing bowl, and microwave on high power for 10 seconds. Add the sugar, cocoa powder, milk, and extract, and beat with an electric mixer at medium speed until fluffy. Spread in the cookie crust and top with ¼ cup of the toffee chips. Freeze for 5 minutes to set. Top with whipped topping, and sprinkle with the remaining toffee chips before serving.

STORAGE NOTE: *Store leftovers in the refrigerator. Do not freeze.*

Microwave Fudge

I have always believed the true value of sweetened condensed milk has been greatly underestimated. Not in this recipe, where it adds sweetness and creaminess to this quick and easy fudge.

Yield: 24 pieces

1 (12-ounce) bag semisweet chocolate chips

1 (14-ounce) can sweetened condensed milk

1 ½ cups chopped walnuts

1 teaspoon pure vanilla extract

Place the chips and milk in a glass mixing bowl, and microwave on high power for 5 minutes. Meanwhile, line an 8-inch square baking pan with parchment paper that has been coated with cooking spray.

Stir the chocolate mixture vigorously, and add the walnuts and extract. Spread evenly in the prepared pan. Place in the freezer for 7 minutes, and then cut into squares.

Storage Note: Store leftovers in the refrigerator in a tightly closed container. Do not freeze.

🕐 *Time-Saving Tip from Tammy*

Parchment paper is a baker's dream because it can withstand temperatures up to 450°. It also makes cleanup a breeze when you use it to line baking pans. Just be careful not to use it under the broiler or with a direct flame because it could ignite.

Strawberries in Warm Vanilla Syrup

This dessert proves you can have an elegant ending to your meal in 15 minutes. While the syrup bubbles away, wash and prepare the strawberries, placing them in stemmed dessert glasses. Don't omit the fresh mint garnish.

Yield: 4 servings

1 cup white grape juice

1 ½ teaspoons lemon juice

¼ cup sugar

1 vanilla bean

1 pint fresh strawberries

Mint sprigs for garnish

In a small saucepan over high heat, combine the white grape juice, lemon juice, sugar, and vanilla bean. As soon as it boils, reduce the heat to medium and simmer for 10 minutes. Meanwhile, hull and slice the strawberries and divide evenly into dessert dishes.

Remove the vanilla bean from the syrup and evenly pour the warm syrup over the strawberries. Garnish with mint sprigs and serve immediately.

STORAGE NOTE: Leftovers can be frozen and used within 4 months or refrigerated and used within 4 days.

Peanut Lovers Dream

It's a triple for those of us who love all things peanut. Look for peanut butter chips in the baking aisle of the supermarket.

Yield: 12 servings

4 tablespoons unsalted butter

¼ cup smooth peanut butter

½ cup packed light brown sugar

24 graham cracker squares

⅓ cup chopped unsalted peanuts

½ cup peanut butter chips

Preheat the broiler on high. Meanwhile, place the butter and peanut butter in a glass mixing bowl and cover with waxed paper. Microwave on low power for 1 to 2 minutes or until the butter has melted. Stir to combine, and add the sugar. Stir constantly until the sugar melts and the mixture is smooth. If necessary, microwave on low power for another 30 seconds.

Place the graham crackers on a parchment-lined jellyroll pan so that the edges are touching. Spread the butter mixture evenly over the crackers. Sprinkle with the chopped peanuts and peanut butter chips. Broil for 1 to 2 minutes or until bubbly. Serve warm.

STORAGE NOTE: Leftovers should be placed in an air-tight container and stored at room temperature. Do not freeze.

Pineapple Orange Cheesecake

*Take a plain, store-bought cheesecake and transform it into
a creation of your own. This recipe was served at a luncheon
I attended, and I loved the fruit combination.*

Yield: 8 servings

2 cups chopped fresh pineapple

2 tablespoons light brown sugar

2 tablespoons unsalted butter

⅓ cup orange marmalade

1 (30-ounce) package plain
  cheesecake (if frozen, thaw)

1 teaspoon rum extract

Whipped cream for garnish

In a medium skillet over medium-high heat, sauté the pineapple, sugar, and butter for 8 minutes. Meanwhile, spread the marmalade over the top of the cheesecake. Remove the pineapple mixture from the heat source, and stir in the extract. Spread over the marmalade. Cut into slices and garnish with the whipped cream. Serve immediately.

STORAGE NOTE: *Refrigerate leftovers tightly covered. Do not freeze.*

🕐 *Time-Saving Tip from Tammy*

I try to never waste food or ingredients. The next time you have leftover whipped cream, just place tablespoon-size dollops on a parchment paper-lined baking sheet. Place in the freezer until firm, and transfer to a zip-top freezer bag. Then you've got "instant" whipped cream to add to hot chocolate or specialty coffee drinks.

Yummy Bananas

Get your ice cream scoop ready for the perfect accompaniment to this dessert. It's deliciously indulgent.

Yield: 6 servings

¾ cup milk

½ cup packed brown sugar

2 tablespoons unsalted butter

2 tablespoons lemon juice

Zest of ½ lemon

½ teaspoon pure vanilla extract

6 bananas

Vanilla ice cream

In a glass bowl, combine the milk, sugar, butter, lemon juice, and zest. Cover tightly with plastic wrap, and cook in the microwave on high power for 2 to 3 minutes. Uncover, and stir in the extract. Set aside.

Peel the bananas and slice in half lengthwise. Arrange in a pinwheel in a round glass baking dish. Pour the vanilla extract mixture over the bananas. Cover with plastic wrap, and cook in the microwave on high power for 5 minutes. Meanwhile, scoop vanilla ice cream into individual serving boats. Uncover the bananas and place on top of the ice cream. Drizzle the sauce over the top and serve immediately.

STORAGE NOTE: Place leftover bananas in a tightly closed container and refrigerate. Do not freeze.

Strawberry Frozen Yogurt

*I experimented with several different frozen fruits before I realized
that the strawberries were by far my favorite. Also, I like the
creamy results from using a blender over a food processor.*

Yield: 4 servings

3 ½ cups frozen strawberries

⅓ cup honey or agave nectar

½ cup plain Greek-style yogurt

1 tablespoon lemon juice

Allow the strawberries to thaw for 10 minutes while measuring other ingredients.
Place the strawberries and honey in a blender, and process until coarsely chopped.
Add the yogurt and lemon juice, and pulse until smooth. Serve immediately.

*Storage Note: Place leftovers in a shallow container and
freeze. After 30 minutes, take a whisk and beat the mixture
well. Return to the freezer for 30 minutes longer, and then
mix mixture again. Use within 1 month for best quality.*

Warm Buttermilk Sauce and Toasted Angel Food Cake

Warm sauces are a dream when served over toasted slices of angel food cake, pound cake, sliced fruit, or homemade vanilla ice cream. Leftovers of this custard-like sauce can be refrigerated for later use.

Yield: 2 ⅓ cups

2 cups buttermilk

½ cup sugar

1 tablespoon cornstarch

3 egg yolks

1 teaspoon pure vanilla extract

6 to 8 (1-inch or larger) slices angel food cake

In a large saucepan, whisk together the buttermilk, sugar, cornstarch, and egg yolks. Place over medium heat and bring to a boil, whisking constantly. Boil for 1 minute, and remove from the heat source. Stir in the extract and set aside.

Set broiler to high. Place the angel food cake slices on an ungreased baking sheet and place under the broiler. Toast until golden brown on one side. Serve with the toasted side up, and generously spoon the warm sauce over the top. Serve immediately.

STORAGE NOTE: Allow leftovers to completely cool; then place a piece of plastic wrap over the top so that it touches the sauce. Refrigerate and use within 4 days. Do not freeze.

🕐 *Time-Saving Tip from Tammy*

For a super-quick dessert, always keep left-over slices of pound cake in your freezer. Then just toast or grill the slices, and top with fresh fruit and whipped cream. If the pound cake seems dry, spread a thin layer of butter on the slices after toasting or grilling.

Cajun Shrimp Toast

This is a great brunch recipe that will soon become one of your favorites. It is traditionally served warm, but if you have leftovers that cool to room temperature, you'll find them just as yummy.

Yield: 20 servings

10 slices white sandwich bread

½ pound cooked salad shrimp

15 water chestnut slices

8 fresh curly parsley leaves

1 small shallot, peeled and quartered

¼ cup soft or whipped cream cheese

2 tablespoons mayonnaise

1 teaspoon Cajun seasoning

¼ teaspoon white pepper

⅛ teaspoon garlic powder

Preheat the broiler. Meanwhile, trim the crust from the bread slices and cut in half diagonally. Place on a jellyroll pan with the sides touching. Broil for 2 minutes or until lightly browned. Remove from the oven to cool slightly, but leave the broiler on.

In the bowl of a food processor, place the shrimp, water chestnuts, parsley, shallot, cream cheese, mayonnaise, Cajun seasoning, pepper, and garlic powder. Process for 30 seconds or until finely minced. Spread evenly over the toasted bread triangles. Broil for 4 to 5 minutes or until lightly browned and bubbly. Serve warm.

STORAGE NOTE: Leftovers can be disassembled. Refrigerate the shrimp mixture and use within 2 days. Discard the toast. Do not freeze.

Fresh Sage and Egg White Pie

This dish is company-worthy. It travels from the stovetop to the oven,
so make sure you use a skillet that doesn't have a wooden or plastic
handle. Any mixture of wild mushrooms will work nicely.

Yield: 6 servings

9 egg whites

3 eggs, lightly beaten

1 cup chopped wild mushrooms

½ teaspoon salt

¼ teaspoon black pepper

2 tablespoons fresh chopped sage

Preheat the oven to 375°F. Coat a nonstick, ovenproof skillet with cooking spray and place over medium heat. Meanwhile, whisk together the egg whites in a mixing bowl until foamy. Add the eggs and whisk well. Stir in the mushrooms, salt, and pepper.

Add the eggs to the skillet and sprinkle the sage on top. Cook for 4 minutes or until the edges are set. Transfer to the oven, and cook for 5 to 6 minutes longer or until set and lightly browned. Serve warm in cut wedges.

STORAGE NOTE: Leftovers should be tightly covered and
refrigerated and used within 2 days. Do not freeze.

🕐 *Time-Saving Tip from Tammy*

If a recipe calls for beaten egg whites to fold into batter, always beat the whites first and set aside. You can use the beaters directly in the other ingredients for mixing the batter. This saves you from having to wash and dry the beaters in the middle of the recipe.

Maple and Chipotle Sausages

I enjoyed these sweet yet spicy sausages at a weekend brunch and have been making them for my own weekend crowds ever since. Start them on the stove as you measure out the other ingredients. Then they can bubble away on the back burner as you prepare the rest of your breakfast or brunch.

Yield: 4 servings

1 (7-ounce) package brown-and-serve link sausages

¼ cup maple syrup

1 teaspoon chipotle peppers in adobo sauce

½ teaspoon garlic powder

¼ teaspoon onion powder

Place the sausage links in a lightly greased skillet over medium heat. Cook for 5 minutes, turning frequently. Meanwhile, in a small mixing bowl, combine the syrup, peppers, garlic powder, and onion powder. Add to the skillet with the sausages and increase the heat to medium-high. Cook for another 5 minutes to glaze the links. Serve warm.

STORAGE NOTE: *Leftovers should be refrigerated and used within 4 days. Or you can freeze for up to 1 month.*

Orange Praline Breakfast Bread

Rather than resorting to plain toasted bread, take a few extra minutes to pop this delight in the oven. It's a taste of New Orleans no matter where you live!

Yield: 6 servings

6 slices French bread

3 tablespoons unsalted butter, softened

⅓ cup packed dark brown sugar

2 tablespoons orange juice

1 tablespoon orange zest

¼ cup chopped pecans

Preheat the broiler to high and place the bread on an ungreased baking sheet. Put under the broiler to toast for 1 minute. Meanwhile, in a small mixing bowl, combine the butter, sugar, orange juice, zest, and pecans. Remove the toast from the oven, and reduce the broiler temperature to low. Spread the butter mixture evenly on the toast slices. Return to the oven and broil for 5 to 6 minutes or until the topping is bubbly. Serve warm.

STORAGE NOTE: You can freeze leftovers for up to 1 month, or refrigerate and use within 3 days. Reheat under a low broiler.

Southern Cucumber Sandwiches

*Don't save these yummy sandwiches just for afternoon tea. They are
equally at home on the brunch bar, particularly during the hot summer
months when supplies of this cool vegetable hit their peak.*

Yield: 4 dozen small sandwiches

1 (8-ounce) package cream
   cheese, softened

½ cup peeled, seeded, and finely
   chopped cucumbers

¼ cup minced green onions

1 tablespoon mayonnaise

1 tablespoon chopped fresh dill

¼ teaspoon salt

¼ teaspoon black pepper

24 slices fresh white bread

In a small mixing bowl, stir together the cream cheese, cucumbers, green onions,
mayonnaise, dill, salt, and pepper. Set aside. Trim the crusts off each slice of the
bread. Spread one side of half the bread with the cucumber mixture. Top with the
other half and cut into triangles with a serrated knife to serve.

*STORAGE NOTE: Leftovers should be disassembled and
refrigerated. Use within 3 days. Do not freeze.*

Warm Cranberry Wassail

This warm winter beverage has the holidays written all over it. Serve it as soon as your guests arrive to knock off the chill and get the party rolling.

Yield: 4 cups

2 cups cranberry juice cocktail

2 cups orange juice or lemonade

½ cup firmly packed light brown sugar

3 whole cloves

2 whole allspice

1 cinnamon stick

In a large saucepan over medium-high heat, bring the cocktail juice, orange juice, sugar, cloves, allspice, and cinnamon to a boil. Stir until the sugar completely dissolves. Reduce the heat to low, and simmer for 5 minutes uncovered. Remove from the heat. With a slotted spoon, remove and discard the spices. Serve immediately.

STORAGE NOTE: Leftovers should be refrigerated and used within 3 days. Gently reheat in the microwave in 30-second intervals.

30 Minutes

Homemade Chicken Nuggets

*Kids aren't the only ones who will flip over these fried favorites. Serve them
with the Tickle Your Tongue Mustard Dip (page 10) for a fun snack or a light
meal. You can save money by cutting boneless, skinless chicken breasts into
cubes rather than purchasing chicken strips or fingers and cutting those.*

Yield: 4 servings

1 cup buttermilk

1 pound boneless, skinless chicken
breasts cut into 2-inch chunks

1 cup panko breadcrumbs

½ cup cornmeal

1 tablespoon grated Parmesan cheese

½ teaspoon garlic salt

½ teaspoon onion powder

½ teaspoon paprika

¼ teaspoon black pepper

¼ teaspoon cayenne, optional

2 tablespoons vegetable or canola oil

Place the buttermilk in a shallow dish, and add the chicken pieces. Cover and allow to
stand at room temperature for 10 minutes.

In a large zip-top bag, combine the breadcrumbs, cornmeal, Parmesan, salt, onion
powder, paprika, pepper, and cayenne, if using. Remove the chicken from the buttermilk (discard the buttermilk), and add to the breadcrumb bag. Shake to evenly coat.

Add the oil to a large skillet and place over medium-high heat. When hot, add the
chicken in a single layer, being careful not to overcrowd the pan. Working in batches
if necessary, cook for 4 minutes on each side or until golden brown and completely
done. Drain on paper towels. Serve warm.

*STORAGE NOTE: Leftovers can be frozen and used within 2
months or refrigerated and used within 4 days. To reheat,
place under a low broiler, turning for even crisping.*

*NOTE: This recipe also works just as well with extra-
firm tofu that has been cut into cubes.*

Crunchy Nut Triangles

I love all kinds of seeds and nuts. They provide the topping for versatile crescent rolls that you can move from the dinner table to the appetizer tray. Feel free to vary the seed and nut selections with what you have on hand.

Yield: 16 servings

1 (8-ounce) can refrigerated crescent rolls

3 tablespoons honey mustard

1 tablespoon bourbon or dark rum

2 tablespoons sunflower seeds

2 tablespoons pine nuts

1 tablespoon sesame seeds

Preheat the oven to 375°F. Lightly grease a cookie sheet with cooking spray and set aside.

Unroll the crescent rolls onto a cutting board and separate the dough into 4 rectangles. Press out the perforations on each rectangle, and cut into 8 triangles per rectangle. Transfer to the prepared cookie sheet, and place so that the triangles are not touching.

In a small bowl, whisk together the honey mustard and bourbon. Evenly brush the mixture over the triangles. In a separate small bowl, combine the sunflower seeds, pine nuts, and sesame seeds. Sprinkle over the top, and bake for 10 to 14 minutes or until golden brown. Serve warm.

Storage Note: Leftovers should be stored at room temperature and used within 2 days. Do not freeze.

🕐 *Time-Saving Tip from Tammy*

The nonskid shelf liners are more than handy in the kitchen. Place a piece in the bottom of a box when transporting cooked dishes, and it will prevent the item from sliding around while driving. Also, put them underneath a cutting board; you will have no movement when slicing.

Candied Pumpkin Pecans

When fall comes and the pecan harvest is in full swing, it's also time for pumpkins, so why not marry the two? This incredible appetizer will not last long, so go ahead and double the recipe from the start!

Yield: 4 cups

1 stick (½ cup) unsalted butter, cubed

1 cup sugar

2 teaspoons pumpkin pie spice

2 teaspoons pure vanilla extract

4 cups pecan halves

Place heavy-duty aluminum foil in the bottom of a large jellyroll pan and set aside. Place the butter in a large skillet over medium heat and stir until melted. Add the sugar and stir until it dissolves. Reduce the heat to low, and cook until golden brown, about 15 minutes, stirring occasionally. Stir in the pumpkin pie spice, extract, and pecans. Cook for 2 minutes longer, stirring constantly. Spread the warm nuts onto the prepared pan. Cool for at least 7 minutes before enjoying warm.

STORAGE NOTE: Leftovers should be placed in a tightly closed container and stored at room temperature. Freeze for no more than 2 months.

⊕ *Time-Saving Tip from Tammy*

When a recipe calls for cubes of butter, first cut the cold stick in half lengthwise with a sharp knife. Then cut those two halves in half before slicing across the stick. You've got perfectly cubed butter to use in the recipe. If those cubes need to be at room temperature and you are in a crunch, simply microwave on the defrost setting for no more than 10 seconds.

Bluegrass Beef Sliders

Little hands like little things, and these pint-size burgers are just the thing for kids of any age. The finely chopped mushrooms keep the burgers moist. If your "audience" doesn't like the tang of blue cheese, substitute shredded Monterey Jack. I like serving these on toasted whole wheat bread instead of buns.

Yield: 8 servings

¾ **pound ground beef**

¼ **cup ground mushrooms***

¼ **cup seasoned dry breadcrumbs**

¼ **teaspoon onion salt**

¼ **teaspoon black pepper**

⅓ **cup crumbled blue cheese**

1 **tablespoon vegetable oil**

8 **slices whole wheat bread**

2 **tablespoons mayonnaise**

4 **small lettuce leaves**

Preheat the oven to 400°F.

In a mixing bowl, combine the beef, mushrooms, breadcrumbs, salt, and pepper. On a large piece of waxed paper, divide the mixture into 8 equal portions, then divide each portion in half. Pat each portion into a flat triangle (so the meat will equal a piece of bread cut on the diagonal). On 8 of the triangles, sprinkle the blue cheese evenly. Take the remaining 8 triangles and cover the blue cheese, mashing the sides to completely seal.

Place the oil in a large skillet over medium-high heat. When hot, add the burgers and cook for 4 minutes on each side. Work in batches if necessary. Transfer the burgers to an ungreased jellyroll pan and place in the middle of the oven. Cook for 4 minutes longer or until the burgers are completely done with no pink remaining.

Meanwhile, toast the bread on the bagel setting of the toaster. Cut in half on the diagonal and spread the untoasted sides with the mayonnaise. Add the lettuce leaves and the burgers. Assemble the sliders, and serve immediately.

STORAGE NOTE: Leftover burgers can be frozen and used within 2 months or refrigerated and used within 4 days.

* Use your food processor for this step.

Fresh Asparagus Sunflower Spread

An overabundance of fresh asparagus inspired this super healthy spread. Slather on toasted French bread or hearty crackers.

Yield: 2 cups

¾ pound fresh asparagus, roughly chopped

1 loaf French bread, cut in 1-inch slices

¾ cup packed fresh parsley

⅓ cup unsalted sunflower seeds

¼ cup lemon juice

2 tablespoons orange juice

2 tablespoons olive oil

2 teaspoons honey

1 garlic clove, minced

1 teaspoon black pepper

½ teaspoon onion salt

½ teaspoon crushed red pepper

Preheat the broiler on high. In a heavy saucepan over medium-high heat, bring 1 inch of water to a boil. Add the asparagus, cover, and cook for 5 minutes. Meanwhile, place the bread slices on an ungreased baking sheet and toast under the broiler for 2 minutes or until tops are golden brown. Set aside to cool. Drain the asparagus, and plunge in ice water. After 1 minute, drain again and pat dry with paper towels.

Place the asparagus in the bowl of a food processor, and add the parsley, sunflower seeds, lemon juice, orange juice, oil, honey, garlic, black pepper, salt, and crushed pepper. Process until finely chopped, but not pureed. Transfer to a serving bowl surrounded by the toasted bread slices.

STORAGE NOTE: Leftovers should be refrigerated and used within 4 days. Do not freeze.

Fried Green Tomatoes

These crispy, fried Southern favorites didn't earn a top spot on the appetizer tray for nothing. They must be served immediately either plain or with ketchup, cocktail sauce, or Ranch dressing.

Yield: 6 servings

Vegetable oil

1 egg, lightly beaten

½ cup buttermilk

½ cup self-rising cornmeal mix

½ cup all-purpose flour, divided

½ teaspoon salt

½ teaspoon black pepper

3 large green tomatoes, cut
   into ⅓-inch slices

Pour the oil to a depth of ½ inch in a large cast iron skillet. Place over medium-high heat, and attach a candy thermometer. Bring to 375°F.

Meanwhile, whisk together the egg and buttermilk in a shallow dish. In a separate shallow dish, combine the cornmeal, ¼ cup of the flour, salt, and pepper. Place the remaining flour in a separate shallow dish. Dredge the tomato slices in the flour, then dip in the egg mixture, and finally dredge in the cornmeal mixture.

Fry in batches in the hot oil for 2 minutes on each side or until golden brown. Drain on paper towels and serve immediately.

Storage Note: Leftovers should be refrigerated and used within 2 days. Reheat under a low broiler, turning to evenly crisp. Do not freeze.

Lime-Salted Sweet Potato Chips

Get ready for a new addiction. These zesty chips are just the thing to start off your next party with a little out-of-the-ordinary zip. Serve them with ice cold beer or gallons of sun tea.

Yield: 6 servings

6 cups canola or vegetable oil

2 teaspoons finely grated lime zest

2 teaspoons salt

3 large sweet potatoes, peeled

½ fresh lime

Place the oil in a deep, heavy skillet over medium-high heat, and attach a candy thermometer. Meanwhile, in a small bowl, mix together the lime zest and salt, and set aside. With a vegetable peeler or mandolin, shave as many long strips as possible from the sweet potatoes. When at the end, use a sharp knife to finish slicing as thinly as possible.

When the oil reaches 375°F, add some potato strips and fry in batches for about 1 minute per batch. Make sure you don't overcrowd the skillet. Give the potatoes enough room to freely move around. Remove with a slotted spoon, and drain on paper towels. Repeat with the remaining potatoes. Transfer the cooled chips to a serving bowl, and sprinkle with the lime salt. Just before serving, sprinkle with the juice of the lime.

STORAGE NOTE: *Leftovers should be stored in an airtight container at room temperature. Do not freeze.*

Black and Blue Salad

Main dish salads get dinner on the table fast. This one features a beautiful portion of lean sliced sirloin steak that sits on a nice bed of lettuce and sliced vegetables. The key to success here is to make sure you allow the meat to rest for 10 minutes before slicing. Pair with the Basic Vinaigrette (page 13).

Yield: 4 servings

1 teaspoon chili powder

1 teaspoon paprika

¾ teaspoon ground cumin

½ teaspoon garlic salt

¼ teaspoon black pepper

1 pound sirloin steak, trimmed

6 cups torn Bibb lettuce

¾ cup peeled and thinly
   sliced cucumber

1 cup red bell pepper strips

½ cup thinly sliced shallots

½ cup crumbled blue cheese

2 tablespoons chopped fresh parsley

In a small bowl, combine the chili powder, paprika, cumin, garlic salt, and pepper. Rub all over the steak and let stand at room temperature for 5 minutes.

Coat a grill pan with cooking spray and place over medium-high heat. When hot, add the steak and cook for 5 minutes. Turn and cook for 4 minutes longer or until you have reached the desired degree of doneness. Remove and place the steak on a cutting board. Allow to stand for 10 minutes before cutting across the grain.

Meanwhile, divide the lettuce among 4 serving plates. Evenly top with the cucumbers, bell pepper strips, shallots, and blue cheese. Add the steak strips and garnish with the parsley. Serve with Basic Vinaigrette (page 13).

Storage Note: Leftover steak strips can be frozen and used within 1 month or refrigerated and used within 4 days.

🕐 Time-Saving Tip from Tammy

Instead of using a fork when turning meat, reach for the tongs. Any piercing you make in the meat will allow internal juices essential for moisture to escape. So pull out the tongs to lock out dryness.

Au Gratin Shrimp Chowder

Canned corn and a package of au gratin potatoes assist this hearty chowder to completion in only half an hour. You can substitute canned, drained lump crabmeat for the shrimp if you wish or cooked diced chicken.

Yield: 6 servings

6 bacon strips

1 small sweet onion, peeled and chopped

1 (4.9-ounce) package au gratin potatoes

1 cup boiling water

1 ½ cups milk

1 ¼ cups vegetable or chicken stock

1 (15.25-ounce) can whole kernel corn, drained

1 bay leaf

⅔ cup evaporated milk

¼ teaspoon black pepper

3 cups small salad shrimp

In a large Dutch oven, cook the bacon over medium heat until crisp. Remove to drain on paper towels, and crumble when cool enough to handle.

Meanwhile, increase the heat to medium-high and add the onions to the drippings. Sauté for 1 minute, and add the potatoes, along with the contents of the sauce packet, water, milk, stock, corn, and bay leaf. Reduce the heat to medium and cook for 17 minutes or until the potatoes are tender, stirring occasionally. Reduce the heat to low, and add the evaporated milk, pepper, and shrimp. Heat for 2 minutes longer, and discard the bay leaf. Serve warm.

STORAGE NOTE: Leftovers can be frozen for up to 2 months or refrigerated and used within 2 days.

Sharp-Dressed Broccoli Cheddar Soup

Frozen broccoli is a great item to have on hand. It is transformed into a creamy, satisfying soup when paired with sharp Cheddar cheese. Enjoy!

Yield: 4 servings

2 tablespoons unsalted butter

1 small sweet onion, peeled and chopped

2 garlic cloves, minced

2 tablespoons all-purpose flour

1 (14.5-ounce) can beef stock

1 ½ cups milk

1 (10-ounce) package frozen chopped broccoli

1 teaspoon Dijon mustard

1 teaspoon Worcestershire sauce

¼ teaspoon white pepper

1 cup shredded sharp Cheddar cheese

In a large saucepan over medium heat, melt the butter and add the onion and garlic. Sauté for 5 minutes, stirring frequently. Add the flour and stir until blended. Gradually stir in the stock and bring to a boil. Cook, stirring constantly, for 2 minutes.

Add the milk, broccoli, mustard, Worcestershire sauce, and pepper. Reduce the heat to medium-low and simmer for 8 minutes. Stir in the cheese until completely melted. Serve warm.

STORAGE NOTE: Leftovers should be refrigerated and used within 4 days. Due to cheese separation at low temperatures, it should not be frozen.

Butternut Squash Soup

In the fall, butternut squash reigns as my favorite of the hard-shelled squash varieties that flood the market. This soup is best served in small amounts because it's rich and filling. It's perfect with a green salad and crusty bread.

Yield: 10 to 12 servings

1 large butternut squash, peeled, seeded, and diced

5 cups vegetable stock

1 cup water

3 medium Yukon gold potatoes, peeled and diced

1 large sweet onion, peeled and diced

2 chicken bouillon cubes

2 garlic cloves, minced

¼ teaspoon white pepper

Sour cream for garnish

Fresh chives for garnish

Combine the squash, stock, water, potatoes, onion, bouillon cubes, garlic, and pepper in a large stockpot or Dutch oven over medium-high heat. Bring to a boil, then reduce the heat to medium-low. Cover and simmer for 15 to 17 minutes.

With an immersion blender, puree the mixture until smooth (or in very small batches, puree in a blender). Serve warm with a garnish of sour cream and fresh chives.

STORAGE NOTE: Leftovers should be refrigerated and used within 4 days or frozen and used within 2 months.

🕐 *Time-Saving Tip from Tammy*

Freezer burn happens when the surface of an item in the freezer dries out. This is usually caused by improper wrapping. Although the food is safe to eat, the quality has been diminished greatly. Prevent this by making sure zip-top freezer bags are free of as much air as possible and using only approved freezer containers.

Creamy Cauliflower and Carrot Soup

Don't knock this soup until you've tried it because the ingredients keep it inexpensive and marry quite well together. It is a great meatless meal that will warm you from the inside out. For special occasions, add a garnish of salad shrimp just before serving.

Yield: 6 servings

1 (16-ounce) package frozen cauliflower

1 cup sliced carrots

¼ cup chopped sweet onions

2 cups vegetable stock

½ cup chicken stock

2 cups milk, divided

1 (10.75-ounce) can condensed cream of potato soup

½ teaspoon garlic powder

¼ teaspoon white pepper

4 teaspoons cornstarch

1 cup shredded sharp Cheddar cheese

Cracked black pepper

Place the cauliflower, carrots, onions, vegetable stock, and chicken stock in a large stockpot or Dutch oven over medium-high heat. Bring to a boil; then reduce the heat to medium. Cover and simmer for 6 to 8 minutes or until the vegetables are tender.

Stir in 1 ½ cups of the milk, as well as the soup, garlic powder, and white pepper. In a small bowl, whisk together the remaining milk and the cornstarch until smooth. Very gradually stir the cornstarch mixture into the soup and bring to a boil. Cook and stir constantly for an additional 3 minutes or until slightly thickened. Add the cheese, and stir until completely melted. Ladle into individual soup bowls, and garnish with fresh cracked pepper.

STORAGE NOTE: Leftovers should be refrigerated and used within 4 days or frozen and used within 2 months.

Get Well Soup

This terrific basic soup was what my mother always wanted when she was feeling bad. Just looking at the recipe, it seems almost forgettable until you try it. Now I crave it, too, with the occasional addition of crumbled blue cheese (see note below).

Yield: 2 servings

2 ½ cups chicken or vegetable stock

8 celery stalks, finely chopped

2 cups milk, room temperature

2 tablespoons unsalted butter

½ teaspoon seasoned salt

¼ teaspoon black pepper

Saltine crackers

Place the stock and celery in a medium saucepan over medium-high heat. Bring to a boil and cook uncovered for 15 minutes or until the celery is tender. Stir in the milk, butter, salt, and pepper, and return to a boil. Serve warm with saltine crackers.

STORAGE NOTE: Leftovers should be refrigerated and used within 4 days. Do not freeze.

NOTE: One day I stirred in ½ cup of crumbled blue cheese to the mixture when I added the milk. It was fantastic!

Dinner Winner Ham and Bean Soup

Leftover ham is given a dinner face-lift with this colorful soup that is enhanced with refried beans. It's not your traditional bean soup, that's for sure, and it's a great way to get beans into little tummies that think they don't like them!

Yield: 8 servings

1 tablespoon vegetable oil

1 large shallot, peeled and chopped

3 cups cooked cubed ham

2 (16-ounce) cans refried beans

1 (14.5-ounce) can vegetable stock

1 (7-ounce) can whole kernel white corn, drained

1 (7-ounce) can whole kernel yellow corn, drained

1 (4-ounce) can chopped green chilies

½ cup salsa

1 teaspoon Cajun seasoning

⅓ cup lime juice

Fresh chopped cilantro for garnish

Place the oil in a large Dutch oven over medium heat, and add the shallot. Sauté for 4 minutes or until tender. Stir in the ham, refried beans, stock, white corn, yellow corn, chilies, salsa, and Cajun seasoning. Increase the heat to medium-high and bring to a boil. Boil for 1 minute, and reduce the heat to low. Simmer for 5 minutes, stirring occasionally. Stir in the lime juice, and serve warm with a garnish of cilantro.

STORAGE NOTE: Leftovers should be refrigerated and used within 4 days or frozen and used within 2 months. Gently reheat in the microwave for 1 minute, then in 30-second intervals.

New Orleans French Onion Soup

*Whoever originally thought of making an onion soup and topping it with
luscious cheese is a winner in my book. This rendition was served to me
at a ladies lunch, and I loved that it had no stringy cheese mess!*

Yield: 8 servings

4 tablespoons unsalted butter, cubed

1 tablespoon olive oil

1 large purple onion, peeled
   and thinly sliced

1 large sweet onion, peeled
   and thinly sliced

2 (14.5-ounce) cans reduced
   sodium chicken stock

3 cups water

1 (1-ounce) package dry onion soup mix

1 teaspoon Worcestershire sauce

1 teaspoon black pepper

½ teaspoon garlic powder

8 (¾-inch thick) slices French bread

½ cup shredded mozzarella cheese

½ cup shredded Swiss cheese

¼ cup shredded Parmesan cheese

Place the butter and oil in a large stockpot or Dutch oven over medium-high heat. Add
the purple and sweet onions, and sauté for 10 to 12 minutes, stirring frequently. Add the
stock, water, soup mix, Worcestershire sauce, pepper, and garlic powder. Bring to a boil;
then cover and reduce the heat to medium-low. Simmer for 5 minutes.

Meanwhile, preheat the broiler and place the bread slices on an ungreased baking
sheet. Sprinkle evenly with the mozzarella and Swiss cheeses. Broil 6 inches from
the heat source for 2 minutes or until the cheese has melted. Ladle the soup into
individual bowls and sprinkle evenly with the Parmesan cheese. Top with a slice of
the cheese bread. Serve warm.

*STORAGE NOTE: Leftovers should be stored minus the cheese toast in the
refrigerator and used within 4 days. Or you can freeze it for up to 2 months.
Simply duplicate the cheese toast part when reheating to serve.*

Keep It a Secret Macaroni and Cheese

Kids don't have to know everything, and the key to making this macaroni dish a favorite depends on keeping the ingredients a secret. Who knew that a nice light bean puree could be such a great culinary trick? It is just enough to thicken the sauce and is a great use for that small amount of leftovers you have in the refrigerator.

Yield: 4 servings

1 ½ cups elbow macaroni

1 tablespoon olive oil

1 tablespoon all-purpose flour

½ cup milk

½ cup canned white or navy beans, drained, rinsed, and pureed

1 ½ cups shredded sharp Cheddar cheese

4 ounces cream cheese

½ teaspoon salt

¼ teaspoon white pepper

Bring a large pot of water to a boil over high heat. Add the macaroni, and cook according to the package instructions.

Meanwhile, add the oil to a heavy saucepan over medium heat. When hot, sprinkle the flour over the oil and stir constantly for 1 to 2 minutes until the mixture thickens. Add the milk and stir until smooth, for about 4 minutes. Stir in the beans, Cheddar and cream cheese, salt, and pepper. Continue to cook and stir until the mixture is smooth and the cheese has completely melted. Remove from the heat, cover, and set aside.

Drain the macaroni in a colander, and shake slightly to remove any excess water. Transfer to a serving dish, and add the cheese mixture. Stir until the macaroni is evenly coated, and serve warm.

Storage Note: Leftovers should be refrigerated and used within 4 days. Do not freeze.

⏱ *Time-Saving Tip from Tammy*

Do you find yourself out of milk, but need some for a recipe? Just open a can of evaporated milk and reconstitute it with an equal amount of water. The water will help thin out the evaporated milk and create a consistency closer to that of fluid milk. That's also a good reason to have dry milk on the pantry shelf.

Fresh Fried Cauliflower

*Crispy nuggets of fried vegetables are a treat for all ages.
This recipe will make even those "I'm not so sure I like
cauliflower" skeptics convert to the thumbs-up side!*

Yield: 6 to 8 servings

Vegetable oil for frying

1 cup all-purpose flour

1 teaspoon salt

1 teaspoon paprika

⅛ teaspoon baking powder

1 cup plus 2 tablespoons club soda

1 egg, beaten

1 ¼ pounds cauliflower florets

Grated Parmesan cheese

Place 6 inches of oil in a large, deep skillet over medium-high heat. Attach a candy thermometer to the side of the skillet. Meanwhile, in a mixing bowl, combine the flour, salt, paprika, and baking powder. Stir in the club soda and egg, and mix until smooth. When the oil reaches 375°F, dip the cauliflower in the club soda mixture and drop into the hot oil. Be careful not to crowd the skillet, giving plenty of room for the cauliflower pieces to cook.

Fry in batches until the cauliflower is golden brown, for around 8 minutes per batch. Drain on paper towels and sprinkle with freshly grated Parmesan cheese just before serving warm.

*STORAGE NOTE: Leftovers should be refrigerated and used within 2 days.
Reheat under a low broiler, turning for even crisping. Do not freeze.*

Double the Cabbage Coleslaw

Feeding a crowd? Then this is the coleslaw for you. I love the color splash of purple with the green cabbage and the tiny flecks of poppy seeds.

Yield: 12 servings

1 head purple cabbage, shredded

1 head green cabbage, shredded

1 cup plain nonfat Greek yogurt

2 tablespoons lemon juice

2 teaspoons sugar

1 teaspoon salt

½ teaspoon white pepper

2 tablespoons poppy seeds

In a large mixing bowl, combine the purple and green cabbage, tossing gently. In a small mixing bowl, whisk together the yogurt, lemon juice, sugar, salt, and pepper. Spoon over the cabbage mixture, tossing to combine. Sprinkle with the poppy seeds and toss again. Cover and refrigerate for 10 to 15 minutes before serving.

STORAGE NOTE: Leftovers should be refrigerated and used within 3 days. Drain slightly before serving with a slotted spoon. Do not freeze.

Hot Potato Pancakes

You'll find that guests will do a flip over these crispy, crusty dinner sides. The addition of cayenne calls for a garnishing dollop of sour cream to tame the heat.

Yield: 10 pancakes

1 egg

1 tablespoon chopped fresh parsley

½ teaspoon cayenne

½ teaspoon garlic salt

¼ teaspoon black pepper

2 large russet potatoes, peeled and halved lengthwise

1 medium sweet onion, peeled and quartered

¼ cup plain dry breadcrumbs

4 tablespoons vegetable or canola oil, divided

Sour cream for serving

In a mixing bowl, whisk together the egg, parsley, cayenne, garlic salt, and black pepper. Set aside. In the bowl of a food processor fitted with the grating disk, grate the potatoes and onions (or grate on the large holes of a box grater). Add to the egg mixture and toss to combine. Stir in the breadcrumbs and mix well.

Heat 2 tablespoons of the oil in a large skillet over medium heat. When hot, gently drop 5 large spoonfuls of the potato mixture into the skillet. Flatten to create even pancakes and cook for 5 to 6 minutes on each side until browned. Drain on paper towels.

Add the remaining oil to the skillet and repeat when hot. Serve pancakes warm with a dollop of sour cream on each.

STORAGE NOTE: Leftovers can be frozen and used within 1 month or refrigerated and used within 4 days. Reheat under a low broiler, turning for even heating.

Green Beans with Tomatoes and Basil

This is the dish I instantly make as soon as I find myself with a harvest of green beans. I already have vine-ripe tomatoes by then and basil by the armload. I adore the color mix it adds to any plate and the vibrant flavors that practically yell fresh!

Yield: 8 to 10 servings

1 ½ pounds fresh green beans, trimmed and snapped

4 tablespoons unsalted butter, cubed

1 shallot, peeled and thinly sliced

3 garlic cloves, minced

1 tablespoon sugar

1 tablespoon lemon juice

¾ teaspoon salt

¼ teaspoon black pepper

2 cups halved cherry tomatoes

2 tablespoons minced fresh basil

Place the green beans in a large pot of boiling water. Cover and cook for 12 minutes. Meanwhile, in a large skillet over medium heat, melt the butter. Add the shallot and sauté for 4 minutes. Stir in the garlic, sugar, lemon juice, salt, and pepper. Cook for 3 minutes longer.

Drain the beans, and add them to the skillet, along with the tomatoes. Heat for 1 minute, and sprinkle with the basil. Serve warm.

STORAGE NOTE: Leftovers should be refrigerated and used within 4 days. The basil will darken as it is stored, so the color will not be as vibrant when serving the second time around. Do not freeze.

Mock "Fried" Okra

I love it when I can just pop something in the oven and set the kitchen timer. This recipe allows you to get other meal tasks done or simply to join the party outside around the grill.

Yield: 6 servings

3 tablespoons canola or vegetable oil

1 tablespoon unsalted butter, melted

1 cup seasoned dry breadcrumbs

1 pound fresh okra, sliced

Kosher salt

Preheat the oven to 400°F. Lightly coat a jellyroll pan with cooking spray and set aside.

Place the oil and butter in a small bowl and the breadcrumbs in a shallow dish. Working in small batches, dip the okra slices into the butter mixture; then dredge in the breadcrumbs. Arrange in a single layer in the prepared pan. Bake for 15 to 20 minutes or until the crust is lightly browned. Serve warm with a sprinkling of salt.

STORAGE NOTE: Leftovers should be refrigerated and used within 2 days. Reheat under a broiler, turning to evenly crisp. Do not freeze.

Hot Water Cornbread

*In the South, this is considered an expected side dish when serving barbecue.
If you've never had it, imagine a cross between cornbread and pancakes.*

Yield: 6 servings

3 cups water

1 cup plain cornmeal

2 tablespoons all-purpose flour

½ teaspoon salt

1 cup vegetable oil

Place the water in a kettle over high heat and bring to a boil. Meanwhile, combine the cornmeal, flour, and salt in a mixing bowl. Place the oil in a large cast iron skillet over medium-high heat.

Gradually add the boiling water to the dry ingredients and stir well. The batter should be thick. Take 2 tablespoons of the batter and press into the shape of a patty. Fry several at a time in the hot oil for 1 minute. Drain on paper towels and serve warm.

STORAGE NOTE: Leftovers can be frozen and used within 1 month or refrigerated and used within 2 days. Reheat in a 300°F oven in a single layer for 5 minutes.

Simple Hushpuppies

Crispy nuggets of fried cornbread complement any kind of fish and are just about the only side dish you need other than coleslaw. This recipe makes plenty for the whole family, as well as friends.

Yield: 3 dozen hushpuppies

Peanut oil

1 ½ cups self-rising cornmeal

½ cup self-rising flour

½ teaspoon salt

½ teaspoon baking soda

¼ teaspoon cayenne

1 small onion, peeled and chopped

1 cup buttermilk

1 egg

Pour the oil to a depth of 4 inches in a large cast iron pot over medium-high heat. Attach a candy thermometer, and heat to 350°F.

Meanwhile, in a mixing bowl, combine the cornmeal, flour, salt, baking soda, and cayenne. Stir in the onion, tossing gently with the dry ingredients to evenly coat. In a small mixing bowl, whisk together the buttermilk and egg. Add to the dry ingredients and stir until well blended. Drop tablespoons of the batter into the hot oil. Fry for 1 to 2 minutes or until golden brown. Drain on paper towels, and serve warm.

Storage Note: Leftovers can be frozen and used within 1 month or refrigerated and used within 2 days.

🕐 *Time-Saving Tip from Tammy*

Do you find yourself out of self-rising flour, but need some for a recipe? Just make your own by combining 1 cup of all-purpose flour with 1 ½ teaspoons of baking powder and ½ teaspoon of salt.

Spiced Collard Greens

Try to get through any Sunday dinner in the South without a mess of greens on the table. It would be unheard of! This spiced rendition gets a bit of heat from hot peppers, which you can diminish if you want or double if you're brave!

Yield: 6 servings

4 slices bacon, halved crosswise

1 sweet onion, peeled and chopped

1 jalapeño pepper, seeded and chopped

½ cup chicken stock

3 tablespoons cider vinegar

1 tablespoon dark brown sugar

2 pounds collard greens, coarsely chopped

½ teaspoon salt

¼ teaspoon pepper

In a large stockpot over medium-high heat, cook the bacon until crisp. Transfer to paper towels to drain, and reserve the drippings in the pot. Add the onion and jalapeño and cook for 2 minutes, stirring frequently. Stir in the stock, vinegar, and brown sugar. Add the collard greens, and cook, covered, for 15 minutes, stirring occasionally. Meanwhile, crumble the bacon and set aside. When the collards are tender, season with the salt and pepper, and transfer to a serving bowl. Top with the crumbled bacon, and serve hot.

STORAGE NOTE: Leftovers can be frozen and used within 2 months or refrigerated and used within 4 days.

Apple, Bacon, and Cheese Dinner Pies

Individual corn crusts form the basis for these unique entrées. They smell, look, and taste very gourmet. Substitute leftover roasted chicken for the bacon, if desired.

Yield: 4 servings

6 slices applewood smoked bacon

1 (8.5-ounce) package corn muffin mix

⅔ cup all-purpose flour

1 teaspoon paprika

1 egg, lightly beaten

¼ cup milk

2 large Granny Smith apples, cored and thinly sliced

⅓ cup crumbled blue cheese

Preheat the oven to 400°F. Lightly grease 2 baking sheets and set aside.

Meanwhile, cook the bacon in a large skillet over medium heat until crisp. Remove and drain on paper towels. Reserve the drippings, and coarsely crumble the bacon when cool enough to handle.

In a mixing bowl, combine the muffin mix, flour, paprika, egg, and milk to form a dough. Divide into four portions, and put two portions on each of the prepared pans. Press into 7-inch circles with your fingers.

Top each dough circle with a layer of apple slices, leaving a 1-inch border. Fold the edges roughly around the outer edges of the apple slices. Brush the apples and crust with the bacon drippings. Bake for 10 minutes. Top evenly with the blue cheese and reserved bacon. Bake for 7 minutes longer or until the edges are golden brown. Cut in half and serve warm.

STORAGE NOTE: Leftovers can be frozen and used within 2 months or refrigerated and used within 4 days. Reheat in a low, 300° oven or in the microwave.

Bacon Herb Chicken

This recipe came to me from my friend Valerie. She serves it as a regular monthly dish to her family. They beg for it, and so do mine! It will take only once to realize this needs to be on your routine dinner rotation.

Yield: 4 servings

5 slices applewood smoked bacon
¼ cup all-purpose flour
½ teaspoon salt
¼ teaspoon black pepper
⅛ teaspoon white pepper
4 boneless chicken breasts
1 tablespoon unsalted butter

4 garlic cloves, peeled and thinly sliced
1 tablespoon minced fresh parsley, thyme, or rosemary
⅛ teaspoon crushed red pepper
¾ cup chicken stock
¼ cup water
2 tablespoons lemon juice

In a large skillet over medium heat, fry the bacon until crisp. Meanwhile, place the flour, salt, black pepper, and white pepper in a large zip-top bag. Add the chicken pieces one at a time and shake to coat.

Place the cooked bacon on paper towels to drain, and add the butter to the skillet. When melted, add the chicken and fry for 6 minutes on each side or until no pink remains. Meanwhile, crumble the bacon and set aside. Remove the chicken and keep warm.

Add the garlic, parsley, and crushed red pepper to the skillet, and cook for 30 seconds. Increase the heat to medium-high, and add the stock, water, and lemon juice. Bring to a boil and continue cooking until the liquid is reduced by half. Return the chicken to the skillet and heat for an additional minute. Top with the bacon pieces, and serve warm.

STORAGE NOTE: Leftovers can be frozen and used within 2 months or refrigerated and used within 4 days.

Filet Mignon with Cream Sauce

Seared steaks keep the delicious juices inside and the meat nice and moist.
These premium cuts are lifted by a creamy sauce that is out of this world!

Yield: 4 servings

1 tablespoon olive oil

4 garlic cloves, minced and divided

1 teaspoon dried thyme

½ teaspoon black pepper

4 (5-ounce) filet mignons
   (1 ½-inches thick)

2 shallots, peeled and minced

1 cup beef consommé

½ cup heavy cream, room temperature

In a small bowl, combine the oil, 2 minced garlic cloves, thyme, and pepper. Rub the garlic mixture on the steaks. Heat a large nonstick skillet over medium-high heat. When hot, add the steaks and cook for 12 minutes, turning once. Remove from the skillet and keep warm.

Add the shallots and remaining 2 minced garlic cloves to the skillet, and stir constantly for 1 minute. Add the consommé, and reduce for 8 to 10 minutes. Remove from the heat, and stir in the cream. Immediately serve the steaks on a pool of the sauce.

Storage Note: Leftovers can be frozen and used within 2 months or refrigerated and used within 4 days.

🕐 *Time-Saving Tip from Tammy*

Have you ever been standing at the meat case and suddenly are confused by all the options available? Here are the five most tender beef steaks: tenderloin steak (which includes filet mignon), chuck top blade steak, top loin steak, porterhouse (sometimes labeled T-bone) steak, and rib-eye steak.

Chicken-Fried Steak

This beef dish has been satisfying Southerners for eons. It is terrific with gravy, if you desire, but equally delicious topped with steak sauce. A bonus is that cubed steak is typically one of the least expensive steak cuts on the market.

Yield: 4 servings

4 pieces cubed steak

2 teaspoons garlic salt

1 teaspoon black pepper

1 cup all-purpose flour

2 eggs, lightly beaten

¼ cup vegetable or canola oil

Pound the meat with a meat mallet on both sides for 30 seconds. Sprinkle each piece evenly with the salt and pepper. Place the flour in a shallow dish such as a pie pan and the eggs in a separate shallow dish. Dredge the meat on both sides in the flour and place on a large baking sheet. Beginning with the first piece done, dredge the meat again in the flour, then in the egg, and then in the flour again. Return the meat to the baking sheet to sit for 10 minutes before cooking.

Preheat the oven to 250°F. Place the oil in a large cast iron skillet over medium-high heat. When hot, add the meat in batches, being careful not to overcrowd the pan. Cook for 4 minutes on each side. Place on a wire rack over a jellyroll pan, and put in the oven to keep warm while cooking the remaining meat. Serve warm.

STORAGE NOTE: *Leftovers can be frozen and used within 2 months or refrigerated and used within 4 days. Reheat under a low broiler, turning to evenly crisp.*

Creamed Scallops

This decadent meal for two is just right for a special night in front of the fireplace. Plus, it doesn't require loads of time spent in the kitchen.

Yield: 2 servings

1 pound large scallops

¼ cup chicken stock

4 tablespoons unsalted butter, divided

½ teaspoon dried onions

3 teaspoons all-purpose flour

½ cup heavy cream, room temperature

¼ cup shredded Gouda cheese

3 tablespoons dry seasoned breadcrumbs

½ teaspoon paprika

Preheat the oven to 400°F, and lightly grease 2 large (8-ounce) ramekins. Set aside.

Place the scallops, stock, 2 tablespoons of butter, and onions in a medium skillet over medium-high heat. Bring to a boil, cover, and reduce the heat to low. Simmer for 2 minutes or until the scallops are firm and opaque. Remove with a slotted spoon, cover, and set aside.

Increase the heat to high, and bring the same poaching liquid back to a boil. Boil for 3 minutes, and stir in the flour until smooth. Gradually add the cream, and return to a boil. Cook and stir for 1 minute or until thickened. Remove from the heat, and stir in the cheese until melted. Stir in the scallops. Evenly distribute in the prepared ramekins.

In a small glass bowl, melt the remaining butter in the microwave on high power for 1 minute. Add the breadcrumbs, and sprinkle over the top of the scallops. Top evenly with the paprika. Bake for 4 minutes or until golden brown. Serve warm.

STORAGE NOTE: Leftovers should be refrigerated and used within 2 days. Do not freeze.

Crawfish Macaroni and Cheese

The South has been having a love affair with macaroni and cheese for centuries. This version is luxurious and terrifically decadent, using Boursin cheese found in the supermarket deli. You can substitute shrimp for the crawfish if you desire.

Yield: 6 to 8 servings

1 pound elbow macaroni

1 (8-ounce) package garlic and herb Boursin cheese

1 (8-ounce) package cream cheese, cut in pieces

¼ pound (4-ounces) processed American cheese (such as Velveeta), cut in cubes

3 cups half-and-half

½ teaspoon cayenne

½ pound cooked crawfish

½ cup dry seasoned breadcrumbs

Place the macaroni in boiling water and cook for 8 to 10 minutes. Meanwhile, preheat the oven to 375°F, and lightly grease a 3-quart baking dish. Set aside.

In a heavy saucepan over medium heat, combine the Boursin, cream cheese, American cheese, half-and-half, and cayenne. Stir frequently until the cheese completely melts. Stir in the crawfish.

Drain the pasta and place in the prepared baking dish. Add the crawfish mixture, and stir well to blend. Sprinkle the top with the breadcrumbs, and bake for 15 minutes or until bubbly and golden brown. Serve warm.

STORAGE NOTE: Leftovers should be refrigerated and used within 3 days. Do not freeze.

Cheeseburger Macaroni and Cheese

This is a one-skillet meal that doesn't require oven baking. You only need a very large skillet with a lid. It will make you a hero to your kids, and with the addition of a green salad, you've got dinner.

Yield: 6 servings

1 pound ground beef

1 shallot, peeled and chopped

2 cups water

¾ cup chicken stock

⅓ cup ketchup

¼ teaspoon black pepper

2 cups uncooked elbow macaroni

½ pound (8-ounces) processed American cheese, cut in cubes

Place the ground beef in a very large skillet over medium-high heat and brown for 5 minutes or until no pink remains. Drain, and increase the heat to high. Stir in the shallot, water, stock, ketchup, and pepper. Bring to a boil, and add the macaroni. Reduce the heat to medium-low, cover, and cook for 10 minutes. Stir in the American cheese until completely melted. Serve warm.

STORAGE NOTE: Leftovers should be refrigerated and used within 3 days. Do not freeze.

🕐 *Time-Saving Tip from Tammy*

A quick way to skim excess fat off browned meat, soups, and stews is to blot the top with the end piece of a loaf of bread. These pieces are typically discarded anyway (the purpose is to keep the cut pieces fresh).

Crumb-Crusted Snapper

Dry breadcrumbs should always be in your pantry. They have dozens of uses, from a mealtime filler to a crispy coating. Here, they serve as a protective outer layer for snapper, but you can substitute any fish fillets you have on hand.

Yield: 6 servings

6 (5- to 6-ounce) red snapper fillets

3 tablespoons buttermilk

¾ cup plain dry breadcrumbs

3 tablespoons grated Parmesan cheese

1 ½ tablespoons chopped fresh parsley

1 teaspoon lemon pepper

½ teaspoon garlic salt

½ teaspoon onion powder

½ teaspoon paprika

3 tablespoons canola or vegetable oil

Lemon wedges

Place the fillets in a large zip-top bag, and add the buttermilk. Allow to stand at room temperature for 5 minutes. Meanwhile, combine the breadcrumbs, Parmesan, parsley, lemon pepper, garlic salt, onion powder, and paprika in a shallow dish.

Place the oil in a large skillet over medium-high heat. Pull the fillets from the buttermilk bath, and immediately dredge them in the breadcrumb mixture. In batches of 3, fry the fillets in the hot oil for 4 minutes on each side or until the fish flakes easily with a fork. Serve warm with lemon wedges.

Storage Note: Leftovers should be refrigerated and used within 2 days. Reheat under the broiler and turn to evenly crisp. Do not freeze.

⏱ *Time-Saving Tip from Tammy*

To make your own buttermilk from regular milk, place a tablespoon of either lemon juice or distilled white vinegar in a cup measure. Add enough milk to bring the measure to the one cup level. Allow to stand at room temperature for 5 minutes before using.

Creole Catfish Po'Boys

*I enjoyed this handheld feast at the house of a good friend
and bothered her until she gave me the recipe. You will love
the spicy coleslaw that sets this sandwich apart.*

Yield: 4 servings

3 ¾ cups coleslaw mix

½ cup mayonnaise

3 tablespoons cocktail sauce

1 ½ teaspoons Creole seasoning, divided

½ teaspoon poultry seasoning, divided

Vegetable oil

½ cup cornmeal

⅓ cup all-purpose flour

1 teaspoon salt

¼ teaspoon black pepper

⅔ cup buttermilk

4 (6-ounce) catfish fillets

4 hoagie rolls, split in half lengthwise

In a mixing bowl, combine the coleslaw mix, mayonnaise, cocktail sauce, ½ teaspoon of the Creole seasoning, and ¼ teaspoon of the poultry seasoning. Toss well to combine; cover and refrigerate until ready to serve.

Place ¼ inch of oil in a large skillet over medium-high heat. Meanwhile, in a shallow dish, combine the cornmeal, flour, salt, pepper, and the remaining Creole and poultry seasonings. Place the buttermilk in a separate shallow dish.

Dredge the fillets in the buttermilk, then in the cornmeal mixture. Fry in the hot oil for 3 minutes on each side or until the fish flakes easily with a fork. Drain on paper towels.

Place ⅓ cup of the coleslaw on the bottom of a hoagie roll. Top with the hot fillet and an additional ⅓ cup of the coleslaw. Put the top of the bun over the coleslaw, and repeat with the remaining rolls, coleslaw, and catfish. Serve immediately.

*STORAGE NOTE: Leftover catfish should be refrigerated and
used within 2 days. Leftover coleslaw should be refrigerated,
as well, and used within 4 days. Do not freeze.*

Garden Fresh Chicken Stir-Fry

Harvest the garden, and harvest dinner! That's about how quickly this meal comes together. I love the substitution of healthy barley for white rice. You will, too!

Yield: 4 servings

2 cups chicken or vegetable stock

1 cup barley

3 teaspoons canola or
   vegetable oil, divided

1 pound boneless, skinless
   chicken breasts, cubed

1 small purple onion, peeled
   and chopped

1 medium zucchini, chopped

1 medium yellow squash, chopped

3 garlic cloves, minced

¼ teaspoon seasoned salt

¼ teaspoon black pepper

⅛ teaspoon crushed red pepper

2 plum or Roma tomatoes, chopped

1 tablespoon minced fresh parsley

1 teaspoon minced fresh oregano

1 teaspoon minced fresh chives

Bring the stock to a boil over high heat in a medium saucepan. Add the barley, and reduce the heat to low. Cover and simmer for 11 to 12 minutes or until the barley is tender. Remove from the heat and let stand for 5 minutes.

Meanwhile, heat 2 teaspoons of the oil in a large skillet or wok over high heat. Add the chicken, and stir-fry for 3 to 4 minutes or until no longer pink. Remove and cover to keep warm. In the same skillet, add the remaining oil and stir-fry the onions for 3 minutes. Add the zucchini, yellow squash, garlic, salt, black pepper, and crushed red pepper. Stir-fry for 4 minutes longer or until the vegetables are crisp-tender.

Stir in the cooked chicken, tomatoes, parsley, oregano, and chives. Plate the barley on a large serving dish, and top with the chicken mixture. Serve immediately.

STORAGE NOTE: Leftovers should be refrigerated and used within 3 days for the best quality. Do not freeze.

🕐 *Time-Saving Tip from Tammy*

Don't skip over the bulk foods aisle at your local supermarket. While most use it to purchase larger than normal amounts, you can also go the opposite direction and get a small amount. This is especially nice when you aren't sure if you like the item you are purchasing. So instead of buying a large package of something like quinoa, you can experiment with just a cup.

Skillet Beef and Vegetables

*One-dish meals have an appeal that goes beyond easy clean-up.
This one marries frozen vegetables with boneless steak, so it
will satisfy both the meat and veggie lovers in your family. The
potatoes eliminate the need for extra beds of rice or noodles.*

Yield: 4 servings

1 tablespoon sesame or peanut oil

1 pound boneless sirloin steak,
    cut into ¼-inch strips

1 (16-ounce) package mixed
    frozen potatoes, green
    beans, and red peppers

½ cup stir-fry sauce

1 teaspoon cornstarch

¼ teaspoon black pepper

Place the oil in a large skillet over medium-high heat. When hot, add the beef strips and cook, stirring frequently for 5 minutes or until you reach the desired degree of doneness. Drain off any excess fat, but leave the beef in the skillet. Add the vegetables.

In a small mixing bowl, combine the stir-fry sauce, cornstarch, and pepper, mixing well. Pour over the vegetables, and gently stir to combine. Reduce the heat to low and cover. Simmer for 6 to 7 minutes or until the vegetables are crisp-tender. Serve warm.

*STORAGE NOTE: Leftovers should be refrigerated
and used within 4 days. Do not freeze.*

Louisiana Shrimp and Sausage

Use either Cajun or Creole seasoning to make this dish sing the dinner tune. It is stretched by substituting quick-cooking bulgur wheat instead of rice. You'll love the difference it makes!

Yield: 4 to 6 servings

1 cup chicken stock

1 cup bulgur

½ teaspoon chili powder

¾ teaspoon Creole or Cajun seasoning, divided

½ pound smoked sausage, cut into ¼-inch slices

2 teaspoons canola or vegetable oil, divided

1 yellow onion, peeled and chopped

1 green bell pepper, seeded and chopped

2 garlic cloves, minced

1 (16-ounce) can red kidney beans, drained and rinsed

1 (14.5-ounce) can diced tomatoes

½ pound large shrimp, peeled and deveined

½ teaspoon Worcestershire sauce

½ teaspoon hot sauce

Place the stock in a small saucepan over high heat and bring to a boil. Stir in the bulgur, chili powder, and ¼ teaspoon of the Creole or Cajun seasoning. Reduce the heat to low, cover, and simmer for 15 minutes.

Meanwhile, brown the sausage in 1 teaspoon of the oil in a large skillet for 4 minutes. Remove and cover to keep warm. In the same skillet, add the remaining oil, and sauté the onion and green bell pepper for 4 minutes or until tender. Add the garlic, and sauté for 1 minute longer. Stir in the beans, undrained tomatoes, remaining Creole or Cajun seasoning, reserved sausage, shrimp, Worcestershire sauce, and hot sauce. Cook for 4 to 5 minutes or until the shrimp turn pink. Fluff the bulgur with a fork, and place on the bottom of a serving dish. Top with the shrimp and sausage mixture, and serve immediately with more hot sauce, if desired.

Storage Note: Leftovers should be refrigerated and used within 2 days. Do not freeze.

Potato Chip Fried Chicken

Pour out the last of a bag of potato chips. You know, the chips that are a little too crushed to enjoy with your lunchtime sandwich. Transform them into a crispy coating for fried chicken, and you've wasted nothing!

Yield: 4 servings

4 tablespoons unsalted butter

¼ cup vegetable or canola oil

1 ¼ cups all-purpose flour

¾ cup finely crushed potato chips

1 teaspoon chili powder

½ teaspoon paprika

¼ teaspoon black pepper

⅛ teaspoon garlic powder

2 eggs

1 tablespoon water

4 boneless, skinless chicken breasts

Place the butter and oil in a very large cast iron skillet over medium-high heat. Meanwhile, in a shallow dish, combine the flour, potato chips, chili powder, paprika, black pepper, and garlic powder. Set aside.

In a separate shallow dish, combine the eggs and water, beating until blended. Dip the chicken in the egg mixture, then dredge in the flour mixture. Repeat by dipping in the egg mixture and dredging in the flour mixture. Add the coated chicken to the hot skillet, and fry for 10 minutes on each side or until golden brown. Drain on paper towels, and serve warm.

Storage Note: Leftovers should be refrigerated and used within 4 days. Do not freeze.

🕐 *Time-Saving Tip from Tammy*

When frying, use a candy thermometer to measure the temperature. Don't have one? Then drop a cube of bread into the hot oil. If it sizzles and begins to slowly turn brown, the oil is ready for frying.

Quick Chicken and Dumplings

*The amazing appeal of chicken and dumplings has made this dish
a classic, but to cook it the old-fashioned way takes a lot of time.
Here's a version you can have hot and ready in only half an hour.
The dumplings are small, bite-size versions that cook fast!*

Yield: 4 servings

3 cups plus ¼ cup milk, divided

½ cup chicken stock

4 cups cubed cooked chicken

1 (10.75-ounce) can condensed
  cream of chicken soup

¼ cup chopped onions

½ teaspoon garlic powder

¼ teaspoon poultry seasoning

¼ teaspoon black pepper

1 cup baking mix

½ teaspoon chopped fresh chives

½ teaspoon dried parsley

Place 3 cups of the milk, along with the stock, chicken, soup, onions, garlic powder, poultry seasoning, and black pepper, in a large stockpot over medium-high heat. Bring to a boil, stirring occasionally.

Meanwhile, in a small bowl, combine the baking mix, chives, and parsley with the remaining milk. Stir just until moistened. Drop by heaping teaspoons onto the simmering chicken mixture. Cook uncovered for 10 minutes. Then cover and cook for 8 minutes longer or until a cake tester or toothpick inserted in the center of the dumplings comes out clean. Serve hot.

*STORAGE NOTE: Leftovers should be refrigerated
and used within 4 days. Do not freeze.*

Pork Cutlet Sauté

I have long been a fan of cutlets, whether they are from turkey, lamb, veal, or pork. This tender cut cooks quickly and is just right for this elegant main dish.

Yield: 4 servings

3 tablespoons canola or
   vegetable oil, divided

½ cup all-purpose flour

¼ teaspoon black pepper

¼ teaspoon paprika

4 (5-ounce) pork cutlets

2 cups sliced fresh mushrooms

½ cup thinly sliced green onions

2 garlic cloves, minced

½ cup vegetable stock

1 cup beef consommé

½ teaspoon salt

¼ teaspoon dried thyme

1 tablespoon chopped fresh parsley

Heat 2 tablespoons of the oil in a large skillet over medium-high heat. Meanwhile, place the flour, pepper, and paprika in a large zip-top bag. Add the cutlets one at a time, and shake to coat. Fry the cutlets 2 at a time in the hot oil for 3 minutes on each side. Remove and keep warm.

In the same skillet, add the remaining oil and sauté the mushrooms and onions for 3 minutes. Add the garlic, and cook for 1 minute longer. Stir in the vegetable stock, consommé, salt, and thyme, and bring to a boil. Cook, stirring constantly, for 3 to 4 minutes or until slightly thickened. To serve, spoon the sauce over the cutlets and garnish with the parsley.

*STORAGE NOTE: Leftover sauce should be stored separately
from the cutlets. Refrigerate and use both within 4 days
or freeze the cutlets and use within 2 months.*

Pork Tenderloin Strips with Crispy Cabbage

This stir-fry dish anchors the meat on a bed of crispy spiced cabbage rather than the same old rice. I pull out this recipe, given to me by a friend, as soon as I harvest my first head of cabbage from the garden. You'll do the same as soon as it hits the market and repeat it throughout the season. You can substitute turkey tenderloin strips for the pork, if you wish.

Yield: 6 servings

7 teaspoons sesame or peanut oil, divided

1 (20-ounce) package pork tenderloins, cut into ½-inch strips

1 tablespoon cornstarch

1 ¼ cups vegetable or chicken stock

⅓ cup plus 2 tablespoons pineapple, peach, or mango chutney

4 teaspoons soy sauce

1 garlic clove, minced

1 teaspoon five-spice powder

⅛ teaspoon white pepper

6 cups shredded cabbage

1 red bell pepper, seeded and julienned

¼ cup chopped fresh parsley

Place 3 teaspoons of the oil in a large skillet over medium-high heat. Add the tenderloin strips, and cook for 8 minutes or until done. Meanwhile, in a medium bowl, whisk together the cornstarch and stock until smooth. Add the chutney, soy sauce, garlic, five-spice powder, and white pepper. Set aside.

Place 3 teaspoons of the oil in a separate large skillet over medium-high heat. When hot, add the cabbage and sauté for 5 minutes or until crisp-tender.

Place the tenderloin strips on paper towels to drain, and set aside. Add the remaining teaspoon of oil to the tenderloin skillet. When hot, add the bell pepper and sauté for 2 minutes. Stir in the chutney mixture, and bring to a boil. Cook, stirring constantly, for 2 minutes longer or until thickened. Add the tenderloin strips to the mixture and heat for 1 minute more.

Place a serving of cabbage on each plate, and top with the pork mixture. Garnish with parsley and serve hot.

STORAGE NOTE: Leftovers should be refrigerated and used within 2 days; however, the cabbage will diminish in crispness.

Unstuffed Beef and Cabbage

I found this recipe in a notebook that my grandmother kept in her kitchen drawer. It's beautifully simple, filling, inexpensive, and free of the time and work necessary to make traditional cabbage rolls.

Yield: 4 servings

1 pound ground beef

1 large green bell pepper, seeded and chopped

1 large butternut squash, peeled and cubed

6 cups chopped cabbage

1 (11.5-ounce) can spicy tomato juice

1 cup water

1 (1-ounce) package dry beef onion soup mix

1 tablespoon light brown sugar

¼ teaspoon black pepper

½ cup instant brown rice

1 tablespoon chopped fresh chives

In a large stock pot over medium heat, cook the beef, green pepper, and squash for 10 minutes or until the meat is no longer pink. Drain and stir in the cabbage, tomato juice, water, soup mix, brown sugar, and black pepper. Bring to a boil; then reduce the heat to medium-low and simmer, covered, for 10 minutes, stirring occasionally.

Add the rice and cook, covered, for 5 minutes more. Remove from the heat, and let stand for 5 minutes before garnishing with the chives and serving hot.

STORAGE NOTE: Leftovers should be refrigerated and used within 4 days. Do not freeze.

Applesauce and Golden Raisin Cookies

*These cookies are soft, and the golden raisins set them apart from
ordinary oatmeal cookies. Have 4 cookie sheets ready for the
recipe so at least 2 can go into the oven at the same time.*

Yield: 4 dozen cookies

1 (18.25-ounce) box spice cake mix   ½ cup vegetable oil

1 egg   1 cup golden raisins

½ cup applesauce

Preheat the oven to 350°F. Lightly grease 4 cookie sheets and set aside.

In a mixing bowl, blend together the cake mix, egg, applesauce, and oil with a mixer on medium speed for 1 minute. Fold in the raisins.

Drop by rounded tablespoons 2 inches apart on the prepared sheets. Bake for 9 to 12 minutes or until the centers are barely set and light brown. While the 2 sheets bake, drop cookie dough onto the other 2 cookie sheets. Remove the first 2 sheets from the oven and cool the cookies for 1 minute before removing onto a wire rack. Cool for at least 5 minutes before serving warm. Repeat with the remaining sheets.

*STORAGE NOTE: Leftovers should be placed in a tightly
closed container and kept at room temperature.*

Butterscotch Pecan Cookies

*I have always been a fan of butterscotch, and these cookies also
utilize crunchy pecans to add texture and personality. This recipe
uses packaged cake mix to eliminate extra measuring.*

Yield: 4 dozen cookies

1 (18.25-ounce) box white cake mix

2 eggs

⅓ cup unsalted butter, melted

¼ cup light brown sugar

1 ½ cups butterscotch chips

½ cup chopped pecans

Preheat the oven to 350°F.

In a mixing bowl, combine the cake mix, eggs, butter, and brown sugar with an electric mixer on low speed for 1 minute. Fold in the butterscotch chips and pecans. Drop by rounded tablespoons 2 inches apart onto 4 ungreased cookie sheets. Place 2 sheets on each oven rack.

Bake for 13 minutes or until just set in the center, switching the sheets top to bottom halfway through. Cool for 1 minute before removing to wire racks to cool for 5 minutes before serving.

*STORAGE NOTE: Leftovers should be placed in a tightly closed
container and kept at room temperature. Do not freeze.*

Chocolate Roll-Ups

This recipe is insanely delicious, and your whole family will crave it. The best part is that the majority of the work is done in the oven, so you can let the aroma bring everyone to the kitchen!

Yield: 4 rolls

1 (8-ounce) container
   refrigerated crescent rolls

1 cup milk chocolate chips
Powdered sugar

Preheat the oven to 400°F. Meanwhile, unroll the dough onto an ungreased cookie sheet. Separate it into 4 rectangles. Don't separate the dough at the triangle perforations, but gently mash the perforations together. Place ¼ cup of the chips on 1 narrow end of each rectangle. Roll up each jellyroll style and pinch the ends closed. Place it seam side down on the cookie sheet and bake for 18 to 20 minutes or until golden brown.

Cool for 4 to 5 minutes, then sprinkle the tops with powdered sugar. Serve warm or at room temperature.

STORAGE NOTE: Leftovers should be refrigerated and used within 2 days. Do not freeze.

Buttery Oat Shortbread

This is a pan cookie that is cut into squares for serving. It needs nothing for embellishment, but is terrific for accompanying seasonal fresh fruit.

Yield: 12 to 15 servings

⅔ cup unsalted butter

½ cup all-purpose flour

½ cup packed light brown sugar

2 cups quick-cooking rolled oats

1 teaspoon pure vanilla extract

Preheat the oven to 350°F. Meanwhile, melt the butter in a mixing bowl on low power in the microwave for 20 seconds. If not completely melted, continue for another 10 seconds. Stir in the flour, sugar, oats, and extract. When well combined, press into the bottom of an ungreased 9-inch square baking pan. Bake for 18 to 20 minutes or until golden brown. Cool for 5 minutes (or completely if desired) before cutting into servings.

STORAGE NOTE: Leftovers should be placed in a tightly closed container and kept at room temperature. Do not freeze.

Cherry Coconut Bars

In the past, I have varied the dried fruits used in this recipe according to what I find lingering in my pantry. It has been cranberries, pineapple, golden raisins, and even chopped dried apricots. But I keep going back to the cherries and find it is my favorite when combined with the coconut-filled macaroons.

Yield: 24 bars

4 tablespoons unsalted butter, cut in pieces

1 ½ cups crushed macaroon cookies

1 (14-ounce) can sweetened condensed milk

¾ cup dried cherries

1 (10-ounce) package white chocolate chips

Preheat the oven to 350°F. Place the butter in a 13 x 9-inch baking dish and put in the oven to melt as the oven preheats. Meanwhile, crush the cookies and gather the milk, fruit, and chips.

Remove the dish from the oven, and layer the macaroon crumbs on top of the melted butter. Pour the condensed milk over the crumbs. Top with a layer of fruit, then a layer of chips. Do not stir.

Bake for 20 minutes or until the edges are golden. Cool for 5 minutes in the pan (or completely if desired) before cutting into servings.

Storage Note: Leftovers should be placed in a tightly closed container and kept at room temperature. Do not freeze.

Individual Peach Crisps

I love single servings. They always tell me that extra effort went into making the recipe. Here, ordinary canned peaches become a luscious dessert with just a few additions from your pantry.

Yield: 4 servings

2 (15-ounce) cans sliced peaches, drained

5 tablespoons light brown sugar, divided

½ teaspoon ground cinnamon

¾ cup all-purpose flour

3 tablespoons quick-cooking oats

2 heaping tablespoons shredded coconut

4 tablespoons unsalted butter, cubed

Preheat the oven to 400°F. Lightly grease 4 (8-ounce) large ramekins and set aside.

In a mixing bowl, combine the peaches, 2 tablespoons of brown sugar, and cinnamon. Divide evenly among the prepared baking dishes.

In a small mixing bowl, combine the flour, oats, and coconut. Cut in the butter with a pastry blender or 2 forks until the mixture resembles coarse crumbs. Sprinkle evenly over the peaches.

Bake for 15 minutes or until the filling is bubbly and the topping is golden brown.

STORAGE NOTE: Leftovers should be tightly covered and kept at room temperature. Do not freeze.

NOTE: You can also bake this in an 8 x 8-inch baking dish for 23 to 25 minutes, if desired.

Maple Cider Apples

I have lots of recipes using apples, but this is the one I keep pulling back out time and time again. Think of it as an apple tart without the crust. You won't miss it!

Yield: 6 servings

2 tablespoons unsalted butter

4 Gala apples, cored, peeled, and cut into thin wedges

¼ cup lemon juice

4 tablespoons sugar, divided

⅓ cup maple syrup

2 tablespoons apple cider or apple juice

Vanilla ice cream

Preheat the broiler to high, and place the butter in a 13 x 9-inch baking pan to melt while preheating. Meanwhile, in a mixing bowl, toss the apples with lemon juice and 2 tablespoons of sugar.

Tilt the baking pan so the butter is evenly distributed throughout the pan. Arrange the apples in a single layer in the pan on top of the melted butter. Broil for 10 minutes or until the apples are just tender and light golden brown.

Meanwhile, in a small saucepan over medium-high heat, combine the maple syrup and cider.

Sprinkle the apples with the remaining sugar and broil for 2 minutes longer. Serve the apples with a scoop of vanilla ice cream and top with a spoonful of the warm sauce.

STORAGE NOTE: Leftover apples can be refrigerated and used within 4 days. Do not freeze.

Strawberry Shortcake Tarts

Because it's just George and me at our house, I have perfected recipes for two. This one can easily be doubled if you have more than that at your home. The food processor makes this recipe dough perfectly.

Yield: 2 servings

½ cup all-purpose flour

2 tablespoons granulated sugar

¼ cup cold, unsalted butter, cut into small chunks

2 tablespoons milk

½ cup crème fraîche or sour cream

2 tablespoons powdered sugar

½ teaspoon pure almond extract

6 large strawberries, hulled and sliced

Preheat the oven to 375°F.

In a food processor, pulse together the flour and granulated sugar. Add the butter and milk, pulsing until the mixture becomes a crumbly dough, for about 15 seconds. Divide the dough in half and place on a lightly greased baking sheet. With your fingers, press each half of dough into a ¼-inch round.

Bake in the middle of the oven for 7 to 8 minutes or until golden brown. Cool on a wire rack in the pan for 5 minutes. Meanwhile, stir together the crème fraîche, powdered sugar, and extract. Place each tart crust on a serving plate. Evenly spread the crème fraîche mixture on top. Decoratively top with the sliced strawberries and serve.

STORAGE NOTE: Refrigerate leftovers and use within 2 days. Do not freeze.

NOTE: If you are not going to serve immediately, you can allow the crusts to cool completely on the wire rack. You can make the crusts up to one day ahead of serving time.

🕐 *Time-Saving Tip from Tammy*

To core strawberries easily, hold the strawberry with the green top against your palm (just like you're going to eat it) and push a flexible drinking straw into the bottom of the berry and through the top of the green. The entire core, cap, and stem will come out without having to cut off the top.

Warm Poached Apples in Cinnamon Syrup

Go to any respectable meat-and-three in the South, and you'll find some form of cooked apples on the menu. Generally, these are stewed, but in this case, the apples are gently simmered. After serving, save the poaching liquid. It can be reduced over medium heat to yield a fine pancake syrup for the upcoming weekend.

Yield: 6 servings

4 cups apple cider

2 cinnamon sticks

8 whole cloves

1 tablespoon whole allspice

1 tablespoon peeled and thinly sliced fresh ginger

6 large apples, peeled, cored, and cut into slices

Place the cider in a large saucepan over high heat and bring to a boil. Meanwhile, tie the cinnamon sticks, cloves, allspice, and ginger in a piece of cheesecloth. Add to the cider, and slip in the apples as you slice them.

As soon as the liquid comes to a boil, reduce the heat to medium and allow the apple slices to poach for 20 minutes. Remove and discard the spice bag. Remove the apples with a slotted spoon, and serve warm.

STORAGE NOTE: Leftovers should be stored in the refrigerator and used within 4 days. Do not freeze.

NOTE: This is a great do-ahead recipe. After preparing as directed, allow the apples to completely cool in the poaching liquid. Remove and discard the spice bag and refrigerate overnight in the saucepan. You can serve the apples chilled, at room temperature, or gently reheated.

⏱ Time-Saving Tip from Tammy

Cheesecloth is a terrific kitchen item and has multiple uses. Rather than purchasing it at the supermarket, you can save money by finding it at craft stores and using their in-store coupons to reduce the price up to half.

Buttermilk and Gouda Grits

Pair creamy Gouda cheese with tangy buttermilk, and you've got grits with zip. It's terrific for breakfast or brunch, but also as an unusual side dish for roasted chicken.

Yield: 8 servings

4 cups vegetable or chicken stock

1 cup heavy cream

1 teaspoon salt

¼ teaspoon black pepper

2 cups quick-cooking grits

2 cups shredded Gouda cheese

½ cup buttermilk

4 tablespoons unsalted butter, softened

Place the stock, cream, salt, and pepper in a large saucepan over high heat. Bring to a boil and whisk in the grits. Reduce the heat to medium-low, and simmer, stirring occasionally, for 15 minutes or until thickened.

Remove from the heat, and stir in the cheese, buttermilk, and butter. Stir until both the cheese and butter have completely melted and the mixture is well blended. Serve immediately.

STORAGE NOTE: Leftovers should be refrigerated and used within 4 days. Add 2 tablespoons of milk or stock to the mixture prior to reheating to soften the consistency. Do not freeze.

Before Noon Shrimp and Grits

Brunch puts on the glitz when this dinner favorite hits the buffet. You'll find it won't last long thanks to the tempting aroma. Who can resist shrimp?

Yield: 4 servings

2 cups vegetable or chicken stock

½ cup water

1 cup quick-cooking grits

1 tablespoon olive oil

½ medium sweet onion, peeled
   and coarsely chopped

½ cup coarsely chopped red bell pepper

½ cup coarsely chopped orange
   or yellow bell pepper

12 jumbo shrimp, peeled and deveined

¼ cup chopped fresh parsley

1 teaspoon lemon juice

¾ cup shredded Parmesan cheese

½ cup sour cream

¼ teaspoon white pepper

In a large saucepan over medium-high heat, bring the stock and water to a boil. Gradually stir in the grits, and reduce the heat to low. Cook for 6 to 7 minutes or until thickened, stirring frequently.

Meanwhile, place the oil in a large skillet over medium-high heat. Add the onion, red bell peppers, and orange bell peppers. Cook for 1 minute. Add the shrimp, parsley, and lemon juice. Cook for 4 to 5 minutes longer or until the shrimp just turn pink.

Stir the cheese, sour cream, and white pepper into the grits. Transfer to a serving dish, and top with the shrimp mixture. Serve hot.

Storage Note: Leftovers can be refrigerated and used within 2 days. Add a couple of tablespoons of milk, wine, or stock to the grits to loosen and bring to a soft texture before reheating. Do not freeze.

Broiled Honey Lime Pineapple

Fruit as a brunch item is usually a mixed salad, but this one really stands out because it's served warm. In addition, this recipe can move from brunch to dessert with practically no effort at all. Just use it as a topping for scoops of vanilla ice cream.

Yield: 8 servings

1 whole pineapple, peeled, cored, and cut into ¼-inch pieces

6 tablespoons unsalted butter, cut into small pieces

⅓ cup honey

2 tablespoons lime juice

3 tablespoons light brown sugar

Preheat the broiler to low, and place an oven rack 6 inches from the heat source.

Lightly grease a jellyroll pan, and spread the pineapple on the pan and dot with the butter. In a small mixing bowl, whisk together the honey and lime juice. Pour over the pineapple, and sprinkle evenly with the sugar. Broil for 12 minutes, basting every 4 minutes with the pan juices. Serve drizzled with the warm juices.

Storage Note: Leftovers should be refrigerated and used within 4 days. Do not freeze.

Buttermilk Corn Sticks or Muffins

Use the same recipe but vary the pan, and you've got the greatest Southern dinner bread of all time!

Yield: 1 ½ dozen sticks or 1 dozen muffins

2 cups self-rising cornmeal

1 egg, lightly beaten

1 ¾ cups buttermilk

¼ cup vegetable oil

Preheat the oven to 450°F, and place the well-greased cast iron stick pan or muffin pan in the oven while it preheats. Meanwhile, in a mixing bowl, combine the cornmeal, egg, buttermilk, and oil, stirring just until the dry ingredients are moistened.

Spoon the batter into the hot stick pan or muffin pan. Return to the oven and bake for 15 to 18 minutes. Promptly remove from the pan and serve hot.

Storage Note: Leftovers can be frozen and used within 2 months or stored at room temperature and used within 3 days.

🕐 *Time-Saving Tip from Tammy*

Making muffins? Remember that lump batter is what will give you those perfectly rounded tops. So just gently stir the mixture until the dry ingredients are moistened. Don't overmix the batter!

Cream Doughnuts

These doughnuts will enchant you from the first bite, and you will never look at others the same way again. These pastries are filled with a sweet creamy mixture enhanced by chocolate hazelnut spread. Divine!

Yield: 10 doughnuts

Vegetable oil for frying

¼ cup heavy cream

6 ounces cream cheese, softened

⅔ cup chocolate hazelnut spread

2 (10.2-ounce) cans large refrigerated biscuits

Powdered sugar for dusting

Place the oil several inches deep in a deep fryer or a deep cast iron skillet, and bring a deep fry thermometer to 375°F.

Meanwhile, in a mixing bowl, combine the cream, cream cheese, and chocolate hazelnut spread with an electric mixer until smooth. Transfer to a pastry bag, and set aside.

Fry the biscuits a few at a time in the hot oil until golden brown on both sides, for around 3 minutes. Drain on paper towels, and repeat with the remaining biscuits. When the doughnuts are cool enough to handle, push the tip of the pastry bag into the side of each doughnut and fill with the cream mixture. Dust the tops with powdered sugar, and serve immediately.

Storage Note: Leftovers should be refrigerated and used within 1 day. Do not freeze.

Grape Tomato and Herb Mini Pies

These beautiful quiches will make guests feel special and will instantly become a centerpiece on the plates. They spotlight a summer harvest of grape tomatoes, as well as snips of herbs from your garden.

Yield: 8 servings

2 cups grape tomatoes, halved

1 ½ cups shredded Monterey Jack or sharp Cheddar cheese, divided

12 eggs

1 cup half-and-half

2 tablespoons chopped fresh chives

1 tablespoon chopped fresh parsley

1 teaspoon chopped fresh oregano or basil

½ teaspoon seasoned salt

¼ teaspoon black pepper

Preheat the oven to 450°F. Lightly grease 8 (6-ounce) ramekins and set on 2 baking sheets. Layer the tomatoes and 1 cup of the cheese evenly in the ramekins. Set aside.

In a mixing bowl with a spout, whisk together the eggs, half-and-half, chives, parsley, oregano, salt, and pepper. Pour the egg mixture evenly into each ramekin. Sprinkle evenly with the remaining cheese.

Bake for 7 minutes, and switch the baking sheets, moving the top sheet to the bottom rack and the bottom sheet to the top rack. Bake for another 8 minutes or until set. Remove the top baking sheet, and place the bottom sheet on the top rack. Bake for an additional 1 to 2 minutes or until lightly browned. Serve warm.

STORAGE NOTE: Leftovers should be refrigerated and used within 2 days. Do not freeze.

NOTE: To make this same recipe in a 13 x 9-inch baking dish, increase the baking time to 18 to 20 minutes or until set.

Lemon Poppy Seed Muffins

I have been making these muffins for years. They taste like they've already been buttered, so they are ready to devour right out of the oven.

Yield: 12 muffins

1 ¾ cups all-purpose flour

½ cup sugar

2 tablespoons poppy seeds

½ teaspoon salt

¼ teaspoon baking soda

1 (8-ounce) carton sour cream

1 egg, lightly beaten

1 stick (½ cup) unsalted butter, melted

2 teaspoons pure lemon extract

Preheat the oven to 400°F. Lightly grease muffin cups, and set the pan aside.

In a mixing bowl, combine the flour, sugar, poppy seeds, salt, and baking soda. Make a well in the center. In a separate small bowl, stir together the sour cream, egg, butter, and extract. Stir into the dry ingredients just until moistened.

Spoon the batter into the prepared pan, filling the cups two-thirds full. Bake for 18 to 20 minutes or until lightly browned. Remove from the pan immediately, and serve warm or at room temperature.

STORAGE NOTE: Leftovers can be frozen and used within 2 months or stored at room temperature and used within 3 days.

🕐 *Time-Saving Tip from Tammy*

The next time you need to melt a stick of butter, use the wrapper to cover the container headed to the microwave. This keeps potential splatter at bay without having to use a piece of waxed paper.

Old-South Buttermilk Biscuits

There is nothing finer than a hot buttermilk biscuit served with any kind of breakfast meat. Then for breakfast "dessert," fill the center with homemade jam or a drizzle of sorghum syrup.

Yield: 2 ½ dozen

4 cups self-rising flour (plus extra for rolling out the dough)

1 cup vegetable shortening

1 ¾ cups buttermilk

Preheat the oven to 425°F. Lightly grease a cast iron biscuit baker or round, flat baking pan and set aside.

Place the flour in a mixing bowl, and cut in the shortening with a pastry blender or 2 forks until the mixture is crumbly. Add the buttermilk and stir until just moistened.

Turn the dough out on a lightly floured surface, and knead lightly 4 times. Roll the dough to ¾-inch thickness, and cut with a 1 ½-inch cutter. Place on the prepared pan, and bake for 13 to 14 minutes or until lightly browned. Serve warm.

STORAGE NOTE: Leftovers can be frozen and used within 2 months or stored at room temperature and used within 2 days.

Peaches and Cream Biscuits

These delightful biscuits are perfect for brunch buffets. They are beautiful, and there's no need to put out extra jams, preserves, or jellies.

Yield: 12 biscuits

3 cups baking mix

1 cup heavy cream

¼ cup peach jam or jelly

2 tablespoons cream cheese, softened

2 teaspoons sugar

Preheat the oven to 400°F. Very lightly grease a cast iron biscuit baker or baking sheet and set aside.

Place the baking mix in a large bowl, and stir in the cream just until moistened. Turn out onto a lightly floured surface, and knead 10 times. Roll out to ½-inch thickness. Cut into rounds with a 2-inch cutter, and place on the prepared pan. Using a teaspoon, make an indentation in the center of each biscuit.

In a small bowl, combine the jam and cream cheese until thoroughly mixed. Drop a teaspoon into the center of each biscuit. Sprinkle the tops with the sugar, and bake for 12 to 15 minutes or until golden brown. Serve warm.

Storage Note: Leftovers should be refrigerated and used within 2 days. Do not freeze.

The South's Best Drop Biscuits

I never liked drop biscuits because they seemed dense and gummy on the inside. Then I decided to experiment until I got it right, and this is the result. You'll have light, airy biscuits every time, and there's no need to knead!

Yield: 12 biscuits

½ cup (1 stick) unsalted butter

2 cups all-purpose flour

2 teaspoons baking powder

1 teaspoon sugar

¾ teaspoon salt

½ teaspoon baking soda

1 cup buttermilk

Place the butter in a glass bowl, and microwave on low power (defrost) for 1 minute. Set aside to cool slightly.

Meanwhile, preheat the oven to 475°F. Lightly grease a jellyroll pan or cover with parchment paper. Set aside.

In a mixing bowl, whisk together the flour, baking powder, sugar, salt, and baking soda. Make a well in the center, and add the buttermilk and melted butter. Stir until the batter has small clumps and pulls away from the sides of the bowl.

Using a ¼ cup measure, scoop level amounts of the batter and drop onto the prepared jellyroll pan about 2 inches apart. Bake for 12 to 14 minutes or until the tops are golden brown. Transfer to a wire rack and cool for 5 minutes before serving warm.

STORAGE NOTE: Wrap leftovers tightly in aluminum foil and store at room temperature. Reheat them in a 300°F oven for 10 minutes. Or you can freeze the leftovers for up to 1 month. Thaw and reheat as directed.

Pick Your Herb Breakfast Muffins

*My herb garden is a constant delight, and I find myself headed out
the back door to snip from it regularly. This muffin recipe lets you
decide which herb you want to accent, or you can combine several into
a unique mixture. Whatever you have in abundance is perfect.*

Yield: 4 servings

1 cup self-rising flour

2 tablespoons fresh snipped herbs
   of your choice (oregano, chives,
   thyme, basil, or parsley)

½ cup milk

3 tablespoons mayonnaise

2 tablespoons unsalted butter, softened

Preheat the oven to 400°F. Lightly grease the cups of a muffin pan and set aside.

In a mixing bowl, combine the flour and herbs. Make a well in the center, and add
the milk and mayonnaise. Stir until well mixed, and spoon into the greased muffin cups, filling each cup half full. Bake for 18 to 20 minutes or until golden brown.
Immediately remove from the muffin pan and split. Evenly divide the butter among
the hot muffins and serve warm.

*Storage Note: Leftovers can be frozen and used within 2 months
or stored at room temperature and used within 2 days.*

Chocolate Bacon

I love a nice mixture of sweet and salty. This recipe is always a hit on the brunch bar, but it can also be served as a dessert or as a great snack. It doesn't take long to prepare, but allowing enough time for the chocolate to set is the key to success.

Yield: 6 servings

6 slices thick bacon

½ pound chocolate candy coating

Chopped walnuts for garnish

Sea salt for garnish

Place 2 paper towels on a plate and arrange the bacon on top so it is not overlapping. Cover with another paper towel, and microwave on high power for 3 ½ minutes. Remove from the microwave, and set the bacon aside on a baking sheet covered with waxed paper.

Place the candy coating in a glass bowl and cover with waxed paper. Melt on low power (or the defrost setting) for 1 minute. Stir to make sure it is evenly melted. Take a spoon, and doing one strip at a time, evenly cover the bacon slices with the candy coating. Go back with any remaining candy coating and drizzle the tops. Immediately sprinkle half of the tops with the walnuts and the other half with sea salt.

Place the sheet in the refrigerator for 15 minutes to set the chocolate. Serve cold or at room temperature.

STORAGE NOTE: Leftovers should be stored in an airtight container in the refrigerator. Use within 3 days. Do not freeze.

Pumpkin Pancakes with Pecan Butter

I had these lovely pancakes at a breakfast institution establishment in Nashville and immediately tried to recreate them at home. It makes me want to shout, "Bring on fall!"

Yield: 4 servings

1 stick (½ cup) unsalted butter	2 teaspoons baking powder
¼ cup maple syrup	1 teaspoon salt
¼ teaspoon ground cinnamon	2 eggs
⅛ teaspoon ground nutmeg	1 ⅓ cups milk
½ cup chopped pecans	¾ cup canned pumpkin puree
1 ½ cups all-purpose flour	½ cup ricotta cheese
2 tablespoons light brown sugar	

Place the butter in a small saucepan over medium heat. Cook for 8 minutes, stirring occasionally. Remove from the heat, and stir in the syrup, cinnamon, nutmeg, and pecans. Set aside.

Preheat a large greased griddle over medium-high heat. Meanwhile, in a mixing bowl, combine the flour, brown sugar, baking powder, and salt. In a separate bowl, whisk together the eggs, milk, pumpkin puree, and ricotta. Stir into the flour mixture just until moistened.

Drop ¼ cup of the batter onto the griddle, and turn when you begin to see bubbles on the top. Cook until golden brown, and serve warm with the pecan butter.

Storage Note: Leftover pancakes can be frozen and used within 1 month. Leftover syrup cannot be frozen, but can be refrigerated and used within 1 week. Gently reheat in the microwave on low power for 30 seconds.

🕐 *Time-Saving Tip from Tammy*

Quite frankly, the only way to know if your griddle is at the proper temperature for pancakes is to make a small one and look at the results. I usually do this with just a tablespoon of the batter and leave it on the griddle for 1 minute. When I flip it over, if it is nice and evenly golden brown, the griddle has preheated to the proper temperature. If not, wait another minute or two and test again.

Sausage Gravy and Biscuits

This is another version of the Southern breakfast classic that is practically foolproof. It is great for teaching new cooks how to make gravy because success is guaranteed.

Yield: 8 servings

8 to 10 refrigerated Southern-
   style biscuits

1 pound pork sausage

1 cup chopped sweet onions

2 tablespoons unsalted butter

1 (2.75-ounce) package
   country gravy mix

1 tablespoon all-purpose flour

⅛ teaspoon black pepper

1 ½ cups milk

1 cup vegetable or chicken stock

Prepare the biscuits according to the package directions. Meanwhile, cook the sausage and onions in a large skillet over medium heat until the sausage is done and no longer pink. Break the sausage into small pieces with a spatula as it cooks. Drain, and add the butter, gravy mix, flour, and pepper. Gradually add the milk and stock, stirring constantly. Bring to a boil and continue stirring for 1 minute longer until thickened. Serve hot on top of the split biscuits.

STORAGE NOTE: Leftovers should be refrigerated and used within 2 days. Do not freeze.

Extra Time-Saving Tips
from *In a Snap!*

Most active dry yeast will have an expiration date on the package, but it's still easy to test it and see if it is "dead or alive." Bring a cup of water to 110°F, testing with a thermometer. Add 2 teaspoons of yeast, and let it stand at room temperature for 5 to 10 minutes. If it's bubbly and thick or if it has expanded, the yeast is still good and can be used. If it hasn't changed much or none at all, the yeast is dead and needs to be replaced.

Unfrosted cupcakes can be individually wrapped in plastic and frozen in a heavy-duty zip-top bag for up to 1 month. Just thaw at room temperature or in the refrigerator, spread with frosting, and serve.

Cake layers need to cool in the pan for 10 minutes after removing them from the oven. That's not the case with cupcakes, which need to be removed from the muffin tin immediately after baking. This applies whether they are cooked in paper baking cups or not. Allow them to cool completely on a wire rack before frosting.

Store-bought taco shells can be heated quickly by hanging them upside down on the bars of your oven rack.

I love waffles, but like to have the family eat at the same time. The solution is to place the cooked waffles on a wire rack placed over a baking sheet. Pop it in a preheated 400-degree oven for 3 to 5 minutes, and you've got crisp, warm waffles for everyone at once.

Pie shields are designed to protect pie crusts from getting too brown during the baking process. If you don't have some, just take out the bottom of a two-piece tart pan. Turn the tart pan upside down over the pie, and the center will be open and continue to cook, but the edges will be shielded from over-browning.

Whenever you rehydrate any dried vegetable, such as dried mushrooms or tomatoes, save the soaking liquid. It makes a great addition to soups, sauces, and stews. Just freeze it in ice cube trays until hard, and then transfer to a labeled zip-top freezer bag.

Let's face it, mixing together the ingredients for meatloaf can be a messy job for your hands. A "less mess" solution is to place all of the ingredients in a large zip-top bag. Then you can easily combine the mixture and see when it is ready for the baking pan.

Handheld olive pitters are equally effective for pitting fresh cherries.

At certain times of the year, like the holidays, cookie cutters of various shapes and sizes are frequently used. They should always be hand washed, but drying them with a towel can be time consuming. Instead, place the clean cutters on a jelly roll pan and place it in the oven that is cooling from cookie baking. They will be dry in just a few minutes and ready to store for the next cookie craze.

A pastry blender makes quick work of chopping boiled eggs for egg salad, for mashing avocados when making guacamole, and for chopping canned whole tomatoes.

Acknowledgments

So many people have made this cookbook a possibility, starting with the fine professionals at Thomas Nelson. They are a writer's dream with vision that is unequaled. Heather Skelton, in particular, is a master and I dearly love her fierce attention to detail and delightful sense of humor. I smile just thinking of her! Mark Boughton, together with Teresa Blackburn, brings photographic genius to the book, with culinary heart and soul in each and every picture. They are trusted and dear friends that I truly treasure. I could work with them every single day and never tire of the task. Bryan Curtis is so valuable to me, I can hardly write the words. He is incredibly patient and kind and brilliant. He balances me with what seems like little effort, but I know the work he pours into each cookbook. Bryan, you are the best!

My taste testers deserve awards. They tirelessly analyze each bite and give me honest, useful feedback that is greatly appreciated. You'll see their work on each page. And to my priceless husband, George, I am beyond grateful. He is my steady rock and shows me daily what love looks like. I honor him, adore him, cherish him, and madly love him. My Grandmother used to always say, "Half of being blessed is knowing you are." I am very blessed!

About the Author

Tammy Algood is a food personality on Nashville's ABC, CBS, NBC, and Fox affiliates as well as statewide on PBS. She has a weekly newspaper column in *The Tennessean* and has recipes featured monthly in *Tennessee Magazine*. She is the author of *Farm Fresh Southern Cooking* and *The Complete Southern Cookbook* and is a marketing specialist with the Tennessee Department of Agriculture.

Index